yOung
Exceptional
children

Monograph Series No. 4

Assessment:
Gathering Meaningful
Information

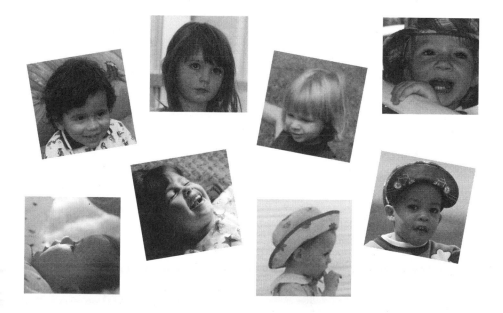

THE DIVISION FOR EARLY CHILDHOOD
OF THE COUNCIL FOR EXCEPTIONAL CHILDREN

Michaelene M. Ostrosky and Eva Horn
Co-Editors

W9-AVC-133

Disclaimer

The opinions and information contained in the articles in this publication are those of the authors of the respective articles and not necessarily those of the co-editors of *Young Exceptional Children (YEC) Monograph Series* or of the Division for Early Childhood. Accordingly, the Division for Early Childhood assumes no liability or risk that may be incurred as a consequence, directly or indirectly, of the use and application of any of the contents of this publication.

The DEC does not perform due diligence on advertisers, exhibitors, or their products or services, and cannot endorse or guarantee that their offerings are suitable or accurate.

Copyright 2002 by the Division for Early Childhood of the Council for Exceptional Children. All rights reserved. 05 04 03 02 01   5 4 3 2 1

No portion of this book may be reproduced by any means, electronic or otherwise, without the express written permission of the Division for Early Childhood.

ISSN 1096-2506 • ISBN 1-57035-809-5

Printed in the United States of America

Published and Distributed by:

SOPRIS WEST
4093 Specialty Place • Longmont, CO 80504
(303) 651-2829 • FAX (303) 776-5934
www.sopriswest.com

634 Eddy Avenue • Missoula, MT 59812-6696
(406) 243-5898 • FAX (406) 243-4730
www.dec-sped.org

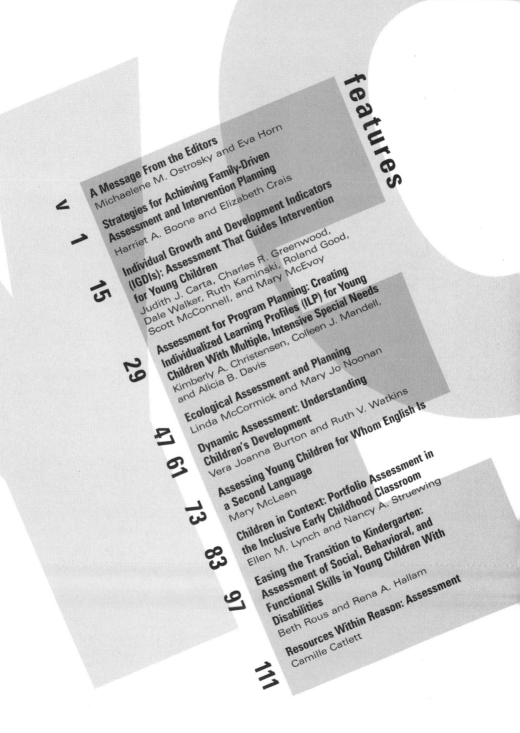

features

A Message From the Editors

Welcome to the fourth issue of the *Young Exceptional Children Monograph Series*. Assessment for young children with disabilities and other special needs is the focus of this issue. The articles in this monograph highlight practices found in Chapter 2 (Neisworth & Bagnato, 2000) of *DEC Recommended Practices in Early Intervention/Early Childhood Special Education* (Sandall, McLean, & Smith, 2000). Bagnato and Neisworth (1991) have defined early childhood assessment as " ... a flexible, collaborative decision-making process in which teams of parents and professionals repeatedly revise their judgments and reach consensus about the changing developmental, educational, medical, and mental health service needs of young children and their families" (p. xi). DEC's recommended practices emphasize: (1) professional and family collaboration, (2) individualized and appropriate assessment, (3) useful information, (4) respectful sharing of information, and (5) meeting legal and procedural requirements as well as recommended practice guidelines. Additionally, the practices are based on the ideas that family members are partners in assessment, the gathering of and interpretation of assessment information must be a true collaborative team process, and that assessment materials must be developmentally appropriate. The articles in this monograph build upon these assessment practices by providing readers with additional information and ideas for gathering meaningful information when conducting assessments in early education settings.

The articles in this monograph build upon these assessment practices by providing readers with additional information and ideas for gathering meaningful information when conducting assessments in early education settings.

The first article, by Boone and Crais, lays a strong foundation for the critical role of collaboration in the assessment process. The specific focus of their article is to ensure that family members, in particular, are involved in all aspects of the assessment and intervention planning for their young child. As noted in the title, the article provides specific "strategies" that practitioners can utilize to support collaborative team assessment for all young children.

Carta and her colleagues from the Early Childhood Research Institute on Measuring Growth and Development (ECRI-MGD) encourage practitioners to focus interventions on meaningful and immediately useful skills that promote positive developmental outcomes for young children. The General Outcomes Measurement (GOM) approach that they describe has been used in other areas of education for more than 20 years to monitor older children's progress (Deno, 1997). Their early education version assists educators in identifying appropriate and meaningful "general outcomes" and implementing procedures for the all-important ongoing monitoring of child progress toward those targeted outcomes.

Christensen, Mandell, and Davis continue the theme of individually appropriate and meaningful information gathering, but shift our focus to young children with multiple, intensive special needs. They describe an approach to information gathering that is grounded in a philosophy of a strengths-based perspective. As part of the Individualized Learning Profile (ILP), these authors present three methods for gathering assessment information and five types of assessment information to be gathered. The importance of understanding how children learn and interact with the environment is a basic premise in this article. Elaborating on this philosophy, in the fourth article McCormick and Noonan describe an ecological assessment and planning process, stressing that behavior cannot be understood without considering the context. This article guides readers in using the process with young children in their care as a method for developing meaningful goals and objectives.

> ...[T]he assessment of young children from culturally and linguistically diverse populations cannot be "business as usual."

Dynamic assessment, with its emphasis on process rather than performance, is the focus of the article by Burton and Watkins. Two forms of dynamic assessment, test-teach-retest and successive cueing, are described in this article. Readers will gain an understanding of how dynamic assessment can provide information about a child's abilities and future development.

McLean challenges practitioners to pause and reflect before moving forward too quickly with assessment and evaluation of young children. Specifically, she reminds readers that the assessment of young children from culturally and linguistically diverse populations cannot be "business as usual." She provides specific culturally and linguistically appropriate strategies to implement across the assessment process, including prior to the initial referral for assessment, to guard against over- or underidentification of children for special education services.

Lynch and Struewing, with their article on portfolio assessment, continue the theme of assessing "children in context." They provide a solid discussion of the value of portfolio assessment for monitoring children's learning and development. As stated in their article, they provide readers with the "nuts and bolts" of information gathering. Through numerous concrete examples and suggestions they provide a very thorough "how to" of the implementation of a portfolio assessment system for practitioners.

Finally, Rous and Hallam discuss the importance of preparing children and families for the transition from an early childhood setting to a school setting. They describe a tool that can be used to assess the functional, social, and behavioral skills of children ages three to six. Readers will find this information helpful in facilitating the development of these important skills.

We hope that as you read the articles in this monograph you are provoked to reflect on and evaluate your current assessment practices. We hope that you find yourself thinking, "I do that," while also considering, "I could try that." Additionally, as you consider the resources described by Camille Catlett in the "Resources Within Reason" section, we hope that you will find new sources of materials to support the gathering, sharing, and use of assessment information in early education.

We extend our sincere thanks to the authors and the reviewers who contributed to this issue of the *Young Exceptional Children* Monograph Series.

Contributing Reviewers:

Janet Bates, University of Kansas
Ann Bingham, University of Nevada-Reno
Patti Blasco, Portland State University
Elizabeth Borreca, University of St. Thomas, Houston, TX
William H. Brown, University of South Carolina
Virginia Buysee, University of North Carolina at Chapel Hill
Lynette Chandler, Northern Illinois University
Kevin Cole, Washington Research Institute, Seattle, WA
Elizabeth Delaney, University of Illinois at Chicago
Janice Fialka, Huntington Woods, MI
Linda Frederick, University of Colorado at Denver
Lise Fox, University of South Florida
Ann Garfinkle, Vanderbilt University
Francis Glascoe, Vanderbilt University
Kristen Greene, University of North Carolina at Chapel Hill
Jennifer Grisham-Brown, University of Kentucky
Moniqueka Gold, Austin Peay State University, Clarksville, TN
Misty Goosen, University of Kansas
Sarah Hadden, University of Wisconsin-Eau Claire
Ann Hains, University of Wisconsin-Milwaukee
Amy Harris-Solomon, Easter Seals Tennessee, Nashville, TN
Joan Houghton, University of Kansas
Jennifer Hurley, University of Kansas
Ronda Jenson, University of Kansas
Hazel Jones, University of Florida

Gail Joseph, University of Colorado at Denver
Toni Ledet, Arkansas' University Center on Disabilities
Chris Marvin, University of Nebraska-Lincoln
Susan Maude, Loras College, Dubuque, IA
Rebecca McCathren, University of Missouri
Mary McLean, University of Wisconsin-Milwaukee
Linda Mitchell, Wichita State University, Kansas
Leslie Munson, Portland State University
Sam Odom, University of Indiana
Missy Olive, University of Texas
Susan Palmer, University of Kansas
Carla Peterson, Iowa State University
Kristi Pretti-Frontczak, Kent State University
Heraldo Richards, Austin Peay State University, Clarksville, TN
Beth Rous, University of Kentucky
Susan Sandall, University of Washington
Rosa Milagros Santos, University of Illinois, Urbana-Champaign
Hannah Schertz, University of Indiana
Barbara Smith, University of Colorado at Denver
Sean Smith, University of Kansas
Patricia Snyder, Louisiana State University Health Sciences Center
Vicki Turbiville, University of Kansas
Mike Wischnowski, University of Rochester
Mark Wolery, Vanderbilt University
Barbara Wolfe, St. Thomas University, Minneapolis, MN
Shih Hua Yang, University of Kansas

References

Bagnato, S. J., & Neisworth, J. T. (1991). *Assessment for early intervention: Best practices for professionals.* New York: Guilford.

Deno, S. (1997). Whether thou goest ... Perspectives on progress monitoring. In J. W. Lloyd, E. J. Kameenui, & D. Chard (Eds.), *Issues in educating students with disabilities* (pp. 77–99). Mahwah, NJ: Erlbaum.

Neisworth, J. T., & Bagnato, S. J. (2000). Recommended practices in assessment. In S. Sandall, M. E. McLean, & B. J. Smith (Eds.), *DEC recommended practices in early intervention/early childhood special education* (pp. 17–27). Longmont, CO: Sopris West.

Sandall, S., McLean, M., & Smith, B. J. (2000). *DEC recommended practices in early intervention/early childhood special education.* Longmont, CO: Sopris West.

Co-Editors: Michaelene M. Ostrosky   Eva Horn
              ostrosky@uiuc.edu   evahorn@ukans.edu

We dedicate this issue of the YEC Monograph Series to our friend and colleague, Mary McEvoy, who passed away on 10/25/02.

Coming next!

The topic for the fifth YEC Monograph is Family-based Practices. For more information, check the DEC Communicator in *Young Exceptional Children* (Volume 6, Number 1) or go to **http://www.dec-sped.org**.

Strategies for Achieving Family-Driven Assessment and Intervention Planning

Harriet A. Boone, Ph.D.,
University of North Carolina at Chapel Hill

Elizabeth Crais, Ph.D., CCC-SP,
University of North Carolina at Chapel Hill

Parent involvement in the educational planning for their child has been supported for more than 20 years. Public Law 94-142, originally passed in 1975, advocated for parents' active and equal participation in their child's educational planning. However, research on the individualized education planning (IEP) process has found that parents typically are not given an active role in their child's educational planning (Gallagher & Desimone, 1995). The Individuals with Disabilities Education Act (IDEA) of 1997 has given professionals the additional impetus to change their practices and further empower parents in their roles as decision makers and advocates for their children via the Individualized Family Service Plan (IFSP). IDEA clearly advocates for family involvement throughout the intervention process. Although recent findings (Mahoney & Filer, 1996; Roberts, Akers, & Behl, 1996) suggest that some programs are adopting family-centered approaches to service delivery, many programs continue to offer families few meaningful choices and allow only limited roles in overall decision making (Crais & Wilson, 1996; Lesar Judge, 1997; Mahoney, O'Sullivan, & Dennebaum, 1990; McBride, Brotherson, Joanning, Whiddon, & Demmitt, 1993).

Obviously, parents play a constant and central role in their child's life (Kjerland & Kovach, 1990). Parents are generally the most reliable and frequent contacts for their child. Parents know their child best. Indeed, research has documented that parents are accurate appraisers of their young child's development, especially when they are asked to make judgments about behaviors their child currently exhibits (Bricker & Squires, 1989; Diamond & Squires, 1993; Henderson & Meisels, 1994).

In order to achieve the family-centered spirit highlighted in IDEA and validated by research findings, professionals must actively collaborate with parents to enhance their ability to be informed decision makers for their child. To facilitate this type of collaboration, the remainder of this article outlines strategies for moving toward an informed family-driven process through preassessment planning, assessment, sharing assessment results, and intervention planning. Two family vignettes representing different family preferences and styles are described in the context of strategies for involving parents in assessment and intervention planning.

Collaborative Preassessment Planning

Parents and children enter the early intervention service system by a variety of routes. For example, parents may refer their child for services, or a family physician or child care provider may initiate a referral. Regardless of how the child and family enter the system, often an important stage in the process is some type of assessment. The assessment is sometimes the family's first encounter with early intervention, so it is extremely important to begin the decision-making process here. Professionals can begin by recognizing that parents know their child best

Vignette

Jamie is a 20-month old with limited expressive language who primarily uses the syllable "da" to express his needs and request the attention of his caregivers. His child care provider and pediatrician both expressed concerns to his mother, who then sought an assessment at a local early intervention program. Jamie's mother was pleased when a professional from the program called to explain the assessment process, its purpose and steps, and to give her several options for participation. Prior to the actual assessment, written information regarding the assessment process, a child history form, and a developmental questionnaire were sent for Jamie's mother to complete and return. The professional then conducted a follow-up call to answer any additional questions and to arrange a meeting date and time. When given the choice, Jamie's mother requested that the assessment team come to their home because she knew Jamie would be more comfortable there. The assessment was planned based on the feedback from the questionnaires and her choices for participation.

and professionals need their direction in planning for a meaningful assessment of the child. Preassessment planning with the family is one means to achieve early collaboration (Crais, 1996b; Kjerland & Kovach, 1990). In the following vignette, the family becomes actively involved in the child's initial assessment through a series of preassessment activities.

There are two purposes of preassessment planning. The first is to introduce the family to the early intervention system. Parents need to understand why an assessment is needed, what information will be gathered and how, who will have access to the information, and how the information will be used (e.g., to determine the child's eligibility for services and/or to assist in planning the child's educational program). This is basic information parents should have at the outset since they are providing very confidential and sometimes sensitive details about their child and family. The second purpose of the preassessment process is to allow parents to introduce their child, their child's development, and their concerns, and to express their preferences regarding the upcoming assessment. Determining the parents' major area(s) of concern, determining what they hope to gain from the assessment, and providing them with choices within the assessment process are just some of the beginning steps.

Regardless of how the child and family enter the system, often an important stage in the process is some type of assessment.

Rather than taking a traditional "deficit" orientation, it may be helpful to have parents first describe their child and the child's strengths. Possible guiding questions may include: "What does your child really like or enjoy?" "What does he or she do well?" "Is there something you want your child to learn or to be able to do differently?" and "Do you have any questions or concerns about your child?" (Crais, 1996a; Kjerland & Kovach, 1990). These types of open-ended questions can help professionals understand the family's concerns and priorities. Commercially available questionnaires include the "Family Interest Survey" (Bricker, 1993) and the "Hawaii Early Learning Profiles Family Centered Interview" (Parks, 1994).

Whether using open-ended questioning or commercially available parent completed questionnaires, it is important to identify the child's interests and areas of strength and capitalize on those as an assessment is planned and implemented. For instance, in Jamie's situation, the professionals learned that Jamie's mother is the primary caregiver and attachment figure. Thus, her presence during the assessment would help Jamie display his most typical and best behaviors. His mother was also very helpful in identifying toys and tasks that she thought would bring out the best in Jamie (e.g., "He loves books and bubbles"). In addition, when she was asked about the order of the tasks that had been identified for use in the assessment, she was especially skillful in knowing which tasks should be tried earlier or later (e.g., "Blocks or things to manipulate with his hands are very frustrating to him, so you may want to do those last"). Thus, parents can work closely with the assessment team to develop the assessment plan and can utilize their knowledge of their child to plan individually "tailored" assessments (Kjerland & Kovach, 1990).

... [I]t is important to identify the child's interests and areas of strength and capitalize on those as an assessment is planned and implemented.

Family-Driven Assessment

To help parents understand the types of participation they may choose during the assessment, it is often useful to describe possible roles. There is a continuum of roles parents may assume, from those that represent more active participation to less active roles (Bailey, McWilliam, Winton, & Simeonsson, 1992; Crais, 1993). Less active roles afford parents the opportunity to be "watchers and listeners" rather than "doers." Some parents prefer this type of role, especially in the beginning when they are unsure of the professionals' expectations. Parent roles that may include somewhat more active participation include describing the child's current skills or demonstrating how they are able to get their child to perform a particular behavior. In Jamie's case, his mother wanted to be actively involved in the assessment in order to interpret his nonverbal communication behaviors and to learn strategies for facilitating his communication. Jamie's assessment was completed in the kitchen of his own home with his mother helping to elicit play and communicative behaviors with the team of professionals. The professionals asked his mother to request certain things from Jamie and to try to engage him in particular play behaviors.

A common example of an active parent role in assessment is provided by the transdisciplinary play-based assessment model (Linder, 1993) in which the parent observes and participates in the assessment simultaneously. This model includes a family facilitator who interprets the arena style play-based assessment for the parent and receives additional insight from the parent regarding the child's behaviors. In this format, the parent can provide the assessment team with suggestions about how to best elicit certain behaviors from the child. Other strategies involve having families complete developmental checklists regarding their child, such as the "Ages and Stages Questionnaire" (Bricker, Squires, & Mounts, 1995), the "Family Report" from the "Assessment, Evaluation and Programming System" (Bricker, 1993), and the "MacArthur Communicative Development Inventories" (Fenson et al., 1993). Some early intervention programs provide parents with an informal questionnaire to complete regarding their child's development in the five primary domains: cognitive, communicative, social, motor, and adaptive. Parents can comment on their child's skills in these areas, any concerns they may have, and what they would like their child to be doing in these areas in six months to a year. A sample form is included in Table 1.

Another way to involve parents in the assessment includes a routines-based (McWilliam, 1992) or activity-based (Bricker, Pretti-Frontczak, & McComas, 1998; Bricker & Woods-Cripe, 1992) approach. This strategy involves having the family and/or child care provider map out the child's daily routines, participation level, and developmental needs in each routine. Some developmental checklists such as the "HELP" (Furano et al., 1979) provide a format for parents to describe and evaluate their child's participation in his or her daily routines. The following vignette describes a routines-based assessment strategy used to involve a mother in her child's assessment.

... [T]he parent can provide the assessment team with suggestions about how to best elicit certain behaviors from the child.

When deciding whether to use a particular strategy or checklist for involving parents, there are some important issues to consider. The overall usefulness of the information requested from parents is vitally important. For example, if an instrument inquires about the family's financial status, and the early intervention program does not have the resources to meet the family's needs in these areas or to assist families in accessing resources, these questions should be omitted. Instead, all information requested should enable the team to design a family-driven intervention plan.

Another consideration concerns the appropriateness or intrusiveness of the information requested. If professionals ask a mother details about her pregnancy and delivery, it is important to explain why that information is needed and how it will help in assessment and intervention planning. Often, professionals ask too much of families, and they do not understand why and what is going to be done with the information. With Will's family, for example, it clearly was inappropriate for the assessment team to question his mother in detail about her pregnancy and delivery since she was reluctant to participate in the early intervention services in the first place and this information wasn't necessary for determining eligibility.

Finally, it is essential to consider the suitability or readability of the language level used in the instrument. Instruments with early intervention jargon such as "pincer grasp," "means ends," or "object permanence" are not user-friendly for most parents. Instruments that

Vignette

Will is a two and a half-year old who lives with his mother and teenage sister. He likes cars, trucks, music, and things that move. His mother operates her own hair styling salon and works 40-plus hours per week. Will goes to a child care center in his neighborhood, but the child care providers there have requested that he be moved to another center unless his behavior can be managed with help from the local health department (Part C agency). Will has trouble adapting to routines, does not interact with his peers, and often engages in very repetitive play. He lives in a community with many children and his mother believes that he should learn to play with children at the child care center and become more a part of their neighborhood community. His mother feels that the child care providers should be able to "handle" Will and resents their requesting help from "outsiders."

After several attempts at reaching Will's mother via telephone, the health department service coordinator sent his mother a letter explaining the services they could provide Will and some information regarding an initial assessment process. Will's mother responded only after the child care providers threatened to kick Will out of the child care center unless his mother consented to an assessment. Will's mother finally consented, but was bitter and angry that she was pushed into something she did not really want. To demonstrate for Will's mother the value of the assessment, the service coordinator began by encouraging her to first describe Will's daily routines and particularly those that were difficult for Will. When comparing his mother's observations with those of his teachers, it became clear that Will was having some of the same types of difficulties at home and at school. Starting with her own observations and the difficulties she was experiencing helped his mother begin to recognize the possible positive results that may come from the assessment and intervention process.

Table 1

Family Preassessment Planning Questionnaire

	What is your child doing now?	What do you want your child to do next?
Moving around		
Using his or her hands		
Thinking about and learning new information		
Relating to other people		
Taking care of his or her own needs		
Understanding what is said to him or her		
Making his or her needs known		
Playing with toys		

give concrete examples or provide pictures of certain skills are often excellent choices for families. Will's mother became involved in the assessment because it was meaningful and useful to her when put in the context of Will's daily routines.

An additional way for families to play an active role in the assessment is to offer them the option of validating the assessment plan, the ongoing assessment activities, and the assessment results. The family can provide the assessment team with valuable feedback about whether particular activities will yield the best behaviors from their child, whether what is observed in the assessment is representative of the child, and their overall impressions of the process and results. Sample questions to encourage validation by families are included in Table 2. Another validating strategy is to share a draft assessment report with parents and ask for their input (Crais, 1993; Kjerland & Kovach, 1990). The family's suggestions or comments can then be incorporated into the final report. For Jamie's assessment, the observations and preliminary findings were discussed by the team and his mother immediately after the assessment. This allowed his mother to ask questions and to answer any remaining questions the professionals had concerning Jamie's behaviors. A draft report was then sent to his mother who shared the report with the child care provider to be certain the behaviors described were typical behaviors for Jamie at home and in his child care environment. His mother then reviewed the report and made comments and suggestions, which were incorporated into the final version.

An additional way for families to play an active role in the assessment is to offer them the option of validating the assessment plan, the ongoing assessment activities, and the assessment results.

Throughout planning and implementing the assessment, it is important to remember the continuum of possible parent roles and attitudes toward assessment. Some parents may want to be actively involved in the planning process whereas others may prefer to know only about the results, and still others may be resistant to any type of assessment. Jamie's and Will's mothers represent a continuum of possible parent roles and attitudes. Jamie's mother was actively involved throughout the process; perhaps her initial awareness that Jamie was having problems communicating helped her see the possible benefits of assessment. Will's mother became involved on a limited basis only after seeing the direct benefit the process may have for her at home. Helping parents become

Table 2

Possible Validating Questions to Ask Families PRIOR to Assessment

- What kinds of information would be most useful to you?
- What kinds of activities or toys would bring out the best in your child?
- What have you or others tried that has been helpful to your child?
- Will the kinds of activities discussed reflect what your child does at home?
- Where and when would be the best place(s) and time(s) to gather information about your child?

Possible Validating Questions to Ask Families DURING Assessment

- Are we getting a representative sample of what your child can do?
- Was that a correct interpretation of what your child just said (or did)?
- How could we approach this task in a way that would help your child feel more comfortable doing it?
- Are there better ways we should be working/playing with your child?

Possible Validating Questions to Ask Families AFTER Assessment

- Did we address your primary concern(s)?
- How do you feel about the overall process and the results?
- Were the behaviors displayed by your child typical for your child?
- What other skills or behaviors does your child do that we were not able to see today?
- What could we have done differently?

Adapted from Crais (1994).

informed consumers of their child's early intervention services means providing them with information and encouraging them to be as active as they want to be in planning, implementing, and interpreting their child's assessment. Parents need to be offered choices throughout the assessment process, and their choices must be honored (Bailey & Blasco, 1990; Crais & Belardi, 1999).

Sharing Assessment Results and Planning Intervention

Assessment results are often used to determine a child's developmental needs and eligibility for services, and to guide the intervention planning process. Thus, the family and professionals must work together not only to gather the information, but also to interpret the assessment results. This stage of the process includes many forms of communication, such as informal information sharing meetings, debriefings, service planning discussions, or staffings (i.e., IEP or IFSP conferences). Typically, one or more of these take place once the assessment is completed. At this point in the process the goal should be cooperative and highly interactive information sharing between parents and professionals (Eiserman, Moore, & Ferguson, 1997). Hopefully, this meeting is characterized by minimal disciplinary boundaries among team members as the family and professionals collectively describe the child. The intent should be to make these meetings proactive and positive—to capitalize on the child's and family's strengths to create a plan for facilitating the child's development.

Collaborative parent-professional information sharing offers many benefits. Most important, it creates a reciprocal and respectful relationship between parents and professionals providing a forum for a true parent-professional partnership. Also, both professionals and parents can learn about alternative perspectives concerning the child's development, which may provide them with additional insight into the child's abilities and needs.

There are several important logistical strategies for achieving a shared view of a child through an interactive sharing process. One is the scheduling and location of the meeting. The time and place should be flexible according to the individual family's needs. Examples of flexibility include having the meeting in the evening or on the weekend so both parents can attend or having the meeting at a parent's place of employment. For example, the intervention planning meeting for Will was held in the supply room of his mother's styling salon. She was not able to leave work to attend the meeting, so the IFSP team arranged to meet her at the salon

Collaborative parent-professional information sharing offers many benefits. Most important, it creates a reciprocal and respectful relationship between parents and professionals providing a forum for a true parent-professional partnership.

during her scheduled break time. Will's mother seemed more comfortable with the professionals at this meeting, perhaps because it was scheduled based on her needs and preferences. If parents are the decision makers for their child, meetings should be held at times and places that are convenient for them. Also, parents should be offered choices about who should be involved in the meetings. Some parents may prefer a minimal number of professionals involved and others may prefer to bring private therapists and/or a family friend to the meeting. Jamie's mother chose to bring his child care provider to the IFSP meeting so that she could contribute to the discussion and understand strategies for working with Jamie on a daily basis.

Professionals typically are well-prepared and often have certain expectations for intervention planning meetings. To ensure parents' full and meaningful participation, it is equally and perhaps more important to prepare them for these meetings. Explaining the intervention planning process and offering parents choices concerning their role in the process are critical. Research has demonstrated that parents' contributions at IEP meetings can be enhanced when they have actively participated in the assessment of their child and have had an opportunity to talk about their own observations (Brinckerhoff & Vincent, 1987). Moreover, the IFSPs of children whose parents had participated in formal IFSP training were more family-centered in the use of lay language and more readily addressed family concerns (Campbell, Strickland, & LaForme, 1992). Table 1 provides a good example of a questionnaire to help parents think about goal setting or next steps for their child.

By beginning with parent-identified issues and concerns, professionals communicate to parents that they are important and their perceptions of their child are important.

Again, parental participation is dependent on the types of choices available and the individual family's preferences. For instance, Jamie's mother chose to be the service coordinator for her child whereas Will's mother chose a professional to coordinate the services and supports.

There are several strategies for preparing parents for the intervention planning process. They include discussing with parents the meeting's purpose, who will be at the meeting, and how they might be involved in the process. It is essential to provide this information to parents in multiple ways as parents are busy and often do not appreciate the full implications of this process unless they can understand the information and how it will impact their child. Jamie's mother was called by the early intervention program's parent facilitator, who was a parent experienced in the assessment and IFSP process. This facilitator explained the process to Jamie's mother and discussed ways she might be involved in addition to sending her written information about the process. Another strategy is to have the child's teacher or service coordinator call or visit the parents several days before the meeting to answer any questions and to have the parents comment on the topics they want discussed at the meeting. Because of Will's mother's busy sched-

Another strategy is to have parents preview the assessment information prior to the meeting to give them an opportunity to organize their thoughts and compile questions concerning their child and the services available.

ule, the early interventionist brought information to his mother about the IFSP two weeks before the scheduled meeting. She also dropped by the salon a week later, in the early morning before any clients arrived, to answer any questions Will's mother had. Another strategy is to have parents preview the assessment information prior to the meeting to give them an opportunity to organize their thoughts and compile questions concerning their child and the services available. Supplementing written information with a verbal explanation and the opportunity for parents to ask questions about the information beforehand is very helpful.

The meeting itself should be organized around parental concerns and parent-identified agenda items. Research has shown that intervention planning meetings are often guided by the form and the required components of the plan, which may interfere with the family-centered intent of these meetings (Able-Boone, 1993; Able- Boone, McBride, Swann, Moore, & Drew, 1998). By beginning with parent-identified issues and concerns, professionals communicate to parents that they are important and their perceptions of their child are important. In addition, asking parents about their child's developmental strengths and needs in particular areas and/or having the parents comment on the child's behaviors in each developmental domain can be useful. Will's IFSP planning was begun by problem solving about difficult routines for him at home that his mother had previously shared. This strategy empowered the mother by acknowledging her concerns and priorities first.

Finally, follow up is essential in realizing true family-centered assessment and intervention planning. Families might be offered the option of having someone from the early intervention team call after the intervention planning meeting to ask if there are any lingering concerns or questions regarding their child and the process. It also is important to share with the parents the steps that have been taken thus far to implement the mutually agreed upon plan. The final assessment report and intervention plan should be given to the parents with their full understanding that both can be modified at any time based on parental concerns.

A Continual Process

Professionals can assist parents in becoming informed decision makers for their child by providing information about every stage of the early intervention process, specifically how parents can be involved based on their individual preferences and how they can shape their child's early intervention program. A summary of strategies for achieving active and informed parent participation are included in Table 3. Professionals and parents continually learn together about a child and how best to meet the child's needs. This process should be ongoing—professionals should continually assess a child and revise their plan based on the child's and family's changing needs. For the process to remain family-driven, parents and professionals need to maintain a reciprocal relationship and periodically update each other about the child's progress. A family-driven philosophy should continue as the child and family proceed through the early intervention system.

Table 3: Strategies for Achieving Active and Informed Family Participation

1. Explain each step of the process via written and verbal communication.
2. Provide the family with choices at every stage of the process.
3. Be willing to meet with the family and child at places and times convenient for them.
4. Provide follow up. Allow families time to review assessment results and the IFSP/IEP and provide opportunities for them to voice their questions and concerns in an ongoing manner.
5. Be flexible based on individual family preferences and styles.

Note
You can reach Harriet A. Boone by e-mail at haboone@email.unc.edu

References

Able-Boone, H. (1993). Family participation in the IFSP process: Family or professional driven? *Infant-Toddler Intervention, 3,* 63–71.

Able-Boone, H., McBride, S., Swann, D., Moore, S., & Drew, B. S. (1998). IFSP practices in two states: Implications for practice. *Infants and Young Children, 10*(4), 36–45.

Bailey, D., & Blasco, P. (1990). Parents' perspectives on a written survey of family needs. *Journal of Early Intervention, 4*(3), 196–203.

Bailey, D., McWilliam, P., Winton, P., & Simeonsson, R. (1992). *Implementing family-centered services in early intervention: A team based model for change.* Cambridge: Brookline.

Bricker, D. (1993). *Assessment, evaluation, and programming system for birth to three years* (Vol. 1). Baltimore: Paul H. Brookes.

Bricker, D., Pretti-Frontczak, K., & McComas, M. (1998). *An activity based approach to early intervention* (Rev. ed.). Baltimore: Paul H. Brookes.

Bricker, D., & Squires, J. (1989). The effectiveness of parental screening of at risk infants: The Infant Monitoring Questionnaires. *Topics in Early Childhood Special Education, 9*, 67–85.

Bricker, D., Squires, C., & Mounts, L. (1995). *The Ages and Stages Questionnaires.* Baltimore: Paul H. Brookes.

Bricker, D., & Woods-Cripe, J. J. (1992). *An activity based approach to early intervention.* Baltimore: Paul H. Brookes.

Brinckerhoff, J., & Vincent, L. (1987). Increasing parental decision making at the individualized educational program meeting. *Journal of the Division of Early Childhood Special Education, 11*, 46–58.

Campbell, P., Strickland, B., & LaForme, C. (1992). Enhancing parent participation in the individual family service plan. *Topics in Early Childhood and Special Education, 11*, 112–124.

Crais, E. R. (1993). Families and professionals as collaborators in assessment. *Topics in Language Disorders, 14*(1), 29–40.

Crais, E. R. (1994). *Increasing family participation in the assessment of children birth to five.* Chicago: Applied Symbolics.

Crais, E. R. (1996a). Applying family-centered principles to child assessment. In P. McWilliam, P. Winton, & E. Crais (Eds.), *Practical strategies for family-centered early intervention* (pp. 69–96). San Diego, CA: Singular.

Crais, E. (1996b). Preassessment planning. *ASHA (American Speech-Language and Hearing Association), 2*, 38–40.

Crais, E., & Belardi, C. (1999). Family participation in child assessment: Perceptions of parents and professionals. *Infant-Toddler Intervention, 9*(3), 209–238.

Crais, E., & Wilson, L. (1996). The role of parents in child assessment: Self-evaluation by practicing professionals. *Infant-Toddler Intervention, 6*(2), 125–143.

Diamond, K., & Squires, J. (1993). The role of parental report in the screening and assessment of young children. *Journal of Early Intervention, 17*(2), 107–115.

Eiserman, W., Moore, S., & Ferguson, A. (1997). *Families and teams together: Improving assessment information sharing and planning process* (Workshop facilitator manual). Boulder, CO: University of Colorado, Division of Speech and Hearing.

Fenson, L., Dale, P., Reznick, J., Thal, D., Bates, E., Hartung, J., Pethick, S., & Reilly, J. (1993). *MacArthur Communicative Development Inventories.* San Diego, CA: Singular.

Furano, S., O'Reilly, K. A., Hosaka, C. M., Inatsuka, T. T., Allman, T. L., & Zeisloft, B. (1979). *Hawaii Early Learning Profile.* Palo Alto, CA: Vort.

Gallagher, J. J., & Desimone, L. (1995). Lessons learned from implementation of the IEP: Applications to the IFSP. *Topics in Early Childhood Special Education, 15*(3), 353–378.

Henderson, L., & Meisels, S. (1994). Parental involvement in the developmental screening of their young child: A multiple source perspective. *Journal of Early Intervention, 18*(2), 141–154.

Kjerland, L., & Kovach, J. (1990). Family-staff collaboration for tailored infant assessment. In E. Gibbs & D. Teti (Eds.), *Interdisciplinary assessment of infants: A guide for early intervention professionals* (pp. 287–298). Baltimore: Paul H. Brookes.

Lesar Judge, S. (1997). Parental expectations of help-giving practices and control appraisals in early intervention programs. *Topics in Early Childhood Special Education, 17*(4), 457–476.

Linder, T. (1993). *Transdisciplinary play based assessment* (Rev. ed.). Baltimore: Paul H. Brookes.

Mahoney, G., & Filer, J. (1996). How responsive is early intervention to the priorities and needs of families? *Topics in Early Childhood Special Education, 16*(4), 437–457.

Mahoney, G., O'Sullivan, P., & Dennebaum, J. (1990). A national study of mothers' perceptions of family-focused early intervention. *Journal of Early Intervention, 14*(2), 133-146.

McBride, S. L., Brotherson, M. J., Joanning, H., Whiddon, D., & Demmitt, A. (1993). Implementation of family-centered services: Perceptions of families and professionals. *Journal of Early Intervention, 17*(4), 414–430.

McWilliam, R. A. (1992). *Family centered intervention planning: A routines based approach.* Tucson, AZ: Communication Skill Builders/Psychological Associates.

Parks, S. (1994). *HELP Family-Centered Interview.* Palo Alto, CA: Vort Corporation.

Roberts, R., Akers, A., & Behl, D. (1996). Family-level service coordination within home visiting programs. *Topics in Early Childhood Special Education, 16*(3), 279-301.

Individual Growth and Development Indicators (IGDIs)

Assessment That Guides Intervention for Young Children

Judith J. Carta, Ph.D., University of Kansas
Charles R. Greenwood, Ph.D., University of Kansas
Dale Walker, Ph.D., University of Kansas
Ruth Kaminski, Ph.D., University of Oregon
Roland Good, Ph.D., University of Oregon
Scott McConnell, Ph.D., University of Minnesota
Mary McEvoy, Ph.D., University of Minnesota

As a home visitor for an Early Head Start program, Ronda visits several infants/toddlers and their families during the course of a week. While the focus of each of these visits varies depending on the child and family needs, the overriding purpose of this early intervention program is to ensure that children's development is on a positive course-that children are making progress toward important outcomes. While Ronda conducts occasional assessments of children who are on her caseload to see where they stand relative to developmental milestones, these assessments don't really help Ronda know whether individual children's progress toward important outcome areas is keeping up with that of other typically developing children. Ronda would really like to be able to identify when a child's rate of progress in an area is not on course compared to other children so she can change or intensify her interventions in that area when that is the case. Yet, at times when Ronda needs to make such a decision, she has few tools at her disposal and usually must rely on her general knowledge of children's development. She thinks she would be more effective if she had some tools that would give her more frequent information about children's progress and that could guide her intervention decisions.

This vignette illustrates what many early interventionists know. While many tools are available for assessing infants and toddlers, persons who work with very young children on a regular basis have limited means of knowing whether their intervention practices are helping a child make progress toward important outcomes. As a field, our emphasis in assessment has been on documenting a delay or diagnosis at the expense of assessing to inform intervention decision making (Meisels & Atkins-Burnett, 2001). Usually, assessments are not conducted often enough to provide practitioners and parents with ongoing information on how a child is doing or whether a program of intervention is working. Existing measures typically are too long and cumbersome to be used at frequent intervals, they often cannot be implemented by the practitioners who need to act on the assessment information, and they generally lack an easy way of tracking rates of growth toward specific meaningful outcomes. Therefore, a gap exists between assessments available and the tools needed to inform practitioners like Ronda who are trying to influence children's progress in early intervention programs.

> *As a field, our emphasis in assessment has been on documenting a delay or diagnosis at the expense of assessing to inform intervention decision making.*

Individual Growth and Development Indicators

Individual Growth and Development Indicators (IGDIs) are measures that can fill the gap by providing helpful information about children's

growth toward outcomes. These new tools for young children are part of an approach to assessment called General Outcomes Measurement (GOM) (Deno, 1997). In this approach, key skill elements that have been specifically linked to important outcomes and selected to represent the domain of interest are measured. A central distinction between this approach and other more traditional assessments (like criterion-referenced testing) is that with GOM, the same set of key skill elements are measured repeatedly over time allowing for the depiction of growth toward identified outcomes. With criterion-referenced testing, on the other hand, a child is assessed on all the specific subskills in a given domain at the child's developmental age.

Examples of a well-known IGDI in the field of pediatrics are children's growth charts (Centers for Disease Control and Prevention, 2000). Repeated measurement and charting of height and weight provides an inexpensive, yet informative means of determining a child's rate of growth toward the important general outcome of normal healthy development (See Figure 1). The graphic record of a child's height and weight plotted over time and compared to children of similar ages easily conveys to the pediatrician and the parents about whether intervention may be needed. This is based not only on the difference between a child's height or weight and those of children of a similar age, but

Individual Growth and Development Indicators (IGDIs) are measures that can fill the gap by providing helpful information about children's growth toward outcomes.

also on the child's *rate of growth* or growth velocity. When a child's rate of growth is lower than age-mates, a pediatrician may consider intervention in the form of improved nutrition or hormonal intervention. Then, the same height and weight charts continue to be used to track rates of growth and the effectiveness of the chosen intervention. While height and weight certainly do not provide a comprehensive measure of a child's general health status, they act as *indicators* of general health. Indicators such as these provide helpful information because they are highly correlated to the general outcome of health and because their ease of use allows them to be used repeatedly and often. Indicators like these are the type of tools that interventionists such as Ronda need to inform them about children's growth in areas other than health.

The General Outcomes Measurement (GOM) approach has been used in other areas of education for more than 20 years to monitor older children's progress in reading (e.g., Shinn, 1989). Frequent quick probes of the number of words a child can read in a short reading passage provide a measure of a child's oral reading rate— an indicator that has proven to be highly related to the more general outcome of reading ability (Deno,

Figure 1: Weight Chart for Girls From Birth to 36 Months From the Centers for Disease Control and Prevention, National Center for Health Statistics

CDC Growth Charts: United States

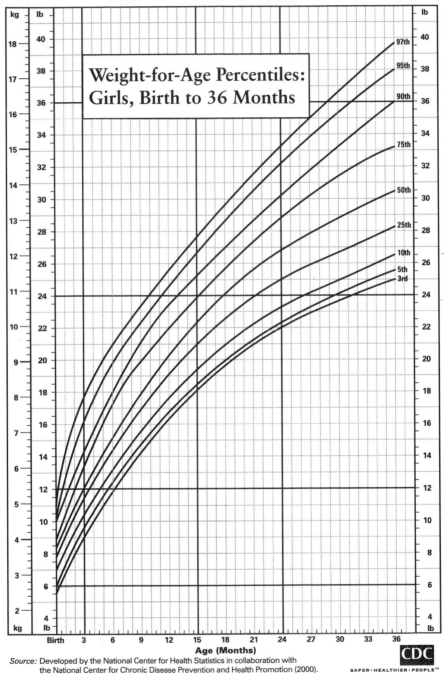

Weight-for-Age Percentiles: Girls, Birth to 36 Months

Source: Developed by the National Center for Health Statistics in collaboration with the National Center for Chronic Disease Prevention and Health Promotion (2000).

Mirkin, & Chaing, 1982). These measures have been demonstrated not only to be reliable and valid but also to be sensitive to instructional intervention (Fuchs & Fuchs, 1986). Therefore, reading rate, when tracked over time, can give a teacher an indication of when a child is falling below expected growth in reading rate, or when specific reading interventions currently being employed are moving a child rapidly toward desired proficiency—just like children's growth charts. In short, the reading rate indicator provides important clues to the teacher about when a change in instruction may be needed to change a child's rate of reading growth. Growth information like this is just what Ronda would find helpful in knowing when to make needed changes in intervention for young children.

Extending the Concept of General Outcomes Measurement to Young Children

IGDIs are GOMs for younger children that have only recently become available (Greenwood, Luze, Cline, Kuntz, & Leitschuh, in press; Luze et al., 2001). Researchers with the Early Childhood Research Institute on Measuring Growth and Development (ECRI-MGD) began the process of developing IGDIs by identifying the general outcomes toward which growth should be measured. Through a national survey of par-

ents and professionals in early childhood and early childhood special education, a list of 15 of the most "socially valued outcomes" for young children was identified (Priest et al., in press). The most highly rated outcome that emerged from this national consensus was the following early communication outcome: "Child uses gestures, sounds, words, and word combinations to express meaning to others." Other general outcomes were identified in self-help/adaptive development, movement, social competency, and cognitive/problem-solving areas.

Specific IGDIs for these outcomes are being developed for children from birth to three years, for children from three to five, and for children from five to eight. For example, to assess infant and toddler growth on the expressive communication outcome described above, a play-like measure that encourages child communication has been developed and validated (Luze et al., 2001). For preschoolers, on the other hand, a more advanced indicator of expressive communication is a measure of children's naming of pictures in a few minutes (McConnell, Priest, Davis, & McEvoy, 2001). Both communication indicators have been demonstrated to be highly correlated to standardized measures of communication and they are also correlated to each other at age three, where the two measures share a common age (Greenwood, 2001).

Example of a Communication IGDI for Infants and Toddlers

The Early Communication Indicator (ECI) (Luze et al., 2001) provides information regarding the number of communication behaviors an infant/toddler exhibits during play with a familiar adult. During a six-minute play period, the infant/toddler is encouraged to play with either a Fisher-Price toy house or barn with a familiar adult caregiver. The role of the play partner is to engage the child with the toy (i.e., the Fisher-Price barn or house) always following the child's lead. The play partner comments generally on the child's play, answers the child's questions, and asks questions based on the child's interest. This partner role by the adult requires some training to be sure the adult is not overly directive in prompting the child to communicate.

During this six-minute play session, another adult records the child's communication behaviors. These are simple tallies (see Figure 2) of each of the following: (1) the child's gestures (the physical movements the child makes during attempts to communicate) (e.g., giving or showing an object, pointing); (2) vocalizations (nonword verbal utterances

voiced by the child (e.g., babbling, laughing); (3) single-word utterances (e.g., "Mine") or multiword utterances (e.g., "That my toy."). At the end of the six-minute play session, the adult who has been recording (the "Coder") sums every category of communication behavior (e.g., gestures, vocalizations, etc.) that occurred during the session and also calculates a total communication score by combining the totals for each separate category of communication behaviors. The rate per minute of total communication is then calculated by dividing the total communication score by six—the number of minutes for the entire play session.

Figure 2: Early Communication Indicator Recording Form Showing Data Recorded During a Six-Minute Play Session

Early Childhood Research Institute **on Measuring Growth and Development**

Expressive Communication
ECI CODING SHEET

Child ID # _Amy_   Wave: _8_
Test Date: _1/7/02_   Assessor: _Ronda_
Coder: _Gabe_   Circle one: (Barn)/ House
Location: _Jayhawk Room_
Reliability (Y) N   Primary Coder Name: _Marla_

	Gestures	Vocalizations	Single Word Utterances (x3)	Multi-Word Utterances (x3)	Total Communication
0:00	G I	V	W	M	1
1:00	G	V IIII	W	M	4
2:00	G I	V I	W	M	2
3:00	G II	V	W	M	2
4:00	G	V	W	M	
5:00	G	V II	W	M	2
TOTAL	4	7			11

Putting the ECI Into Practice

The ECI can be used in home visiting programs, like the one in which Ronda works, or in center-based programs. Because the assessment requires two adults (one to serve as play partner for the child and one to serve as the Coder who records the child's communication behaviors), it 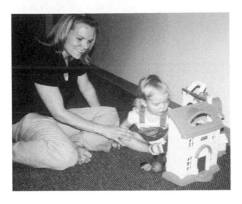 would work best if Ronda, for example, could recruit another adult who can tally the child behaviors while Ronda acts as the play partner during the assessment. While parents or child care providers in centers can serve as play partners, they may need some training to follow the child's lead during the assessment and not engage in a multitude of drill-like questions that may evoke one-word responses. Another alternative, if no additional adult is available, is to videotape the six-minute play session and code the child behaviors from the videotape at a later point.

Using ECI Data to Make Intervention Decisions

A model for making decisions has been created to help practitioners and families use the IGDIs for guiding and adapting interventions (see Figure 3) (ECRI-MGD, 1998). This model is based on similar problem-solving models for using General Outcomes Measurement (e.g., Deno, 1985; Kaminski & Good, 1996) and involves using the IGDIs in four ways: (1) to monitor growth, and (2) to identify when an intervention is needed. Once practitioners have identified a need for intervention, other assessments are used to explore possible intervention solutions to do the following: (2a) generate intervention options, and (2b) implement intervention and measure the fidelity of intervention. Finally, IGDIs are used in the process to: (3) evaluate the child's growth in the course of the new intervention, and (4) continue monitoring the child's progress over time.

For example, Ronda may choose to use the ECI to monitor the growth of communication for the children on her caseload by conducting individual monthly ECI assessments as previously described. Individual scores could then be entered into a specially designed EXCEL template database. Using the EXCEL program, Ronda could generate graphs of any child's total communication score and graphs for each separate category of communication (e.g., single words, multiple words)

Figure 3: Decision-Making Model Using IGDIs to Monitor Progress on Interventions

IGDI Decision-Making Model

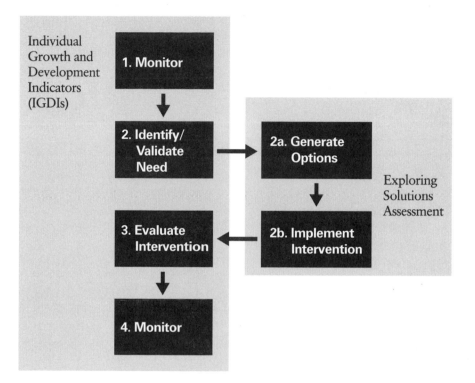

across months. She also could display growth charts summarizing her entire caseload combined, and how the growth of one child or the growth of all the children on her caseload compared to the growth of all children in the Early Head Start program.

In the course of monthly monitoring of all children's communication growth in this way, Ronda noticed that Amy, a 14-month old girl, was producing only between two to three communications per minute per month (see Figure 4) and that her pattern of growth was flat if not declining from one month to the next. Comparing her performance of two or three communications per minute to that of typical children her same age as depicted on the normative aim line (i.e., eight to nine communications per minute), her lack of progress was a concern. Just like a height and weight chart, Ronda could see from Amy's ECI chart that she was not growing in communication skills at the same rate as peers her own age.

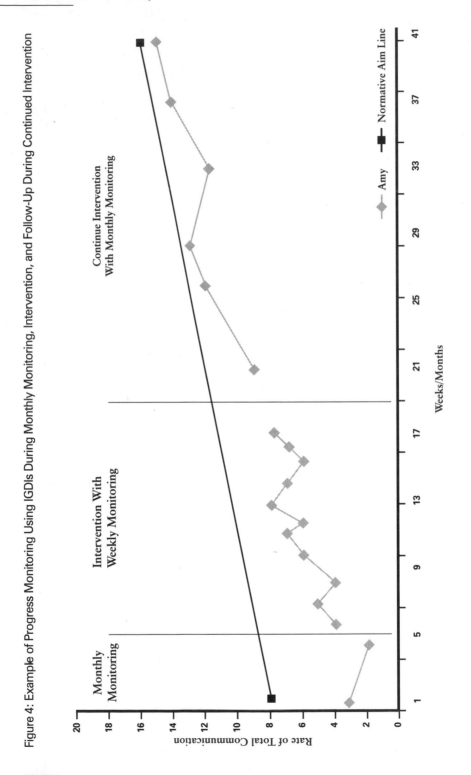

Figure 4: Example of Progress Monitoring Using IGDIs During Monthly Monitoring, Intervention, and Follow-Up During Continued Intervention

Ronda decided to refer Amy for more assessment of her communication, whereupon it was confirmed, based on additional testing, that Amy had a delay in expressive communication. After ruling out possible medical causes, Amy's intervention team (including her parents and child care providers) examined other possible causes for Amy's delay, looking for potential solutions. Through this process, it was noted that Amy spent most of her waking hours in a child care environment where 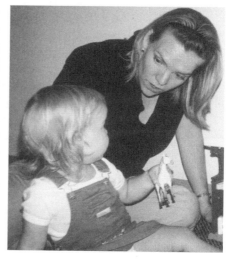 caregivers made little effort to promote her language use. For example, an informal observation indicated that the child care providers gave Amy very few opportunities to communicate and her requests in the child care environment were quickly met with no requirement that she elaborate or expand by using language.

Ronda and the intervention team decided to help Amy's child care providers learn how to promote her expressive communication by following her lead, requiring her to use her limited vocabulary, and by expanding on her utterances. The intervention was implemented intensively on a daily basis for three months, during which time Ronda increased the frequency of the ECI assessments from monthly to weekly so that she would have more data to track Amy's progress in the presence of this focused intervention. Amy's graph showed that during the 12 weeks (three months) of intervention, her rate of progress shot up dramatically and her weekly level of total communication was approaching that of typically developing peers (see Figure 4). Ronda and the intervention team (including the child care providers) used the data to confirm that the intervention was having the desired effect and they projected that if this rate of progress continued, Amy would probably be communicating at a rate similar to typically developing children within the next two to three months. Consequently, the child care providers were encouraged to continue their successful intervention efforts with Amy and with other children under their care. Additionally, based on Amy's progress, the frequency of ECI assessments was cut back from weekly to monthly (see Figure 4).

Using ECI to Monitor Programs

While IGDIs are helpful in monitoring individual children's growth over time, program directors can use the same strategy for measuring growth of all children in their programs. In this

way program directors can use children's growth as an indicator of whether the program is moving children in a timely way toward meaningful outcomes. It is possible that changes in rates of growth in entire programs can be used to indicate how shifts in policies or programs (such as size of caseloads, frequency of home visits, changes in the curriculum) actually affect children. For example, a program director could examine the average rates of growth of all of the children in expressive communication for a six-month period and then continue to track growth after the staff received training on interventions to promote responsive interaction of caregivers on their caseloads. Comparing rates of growth on the ECI for a period of time before and after training on this intervention would provide helpful information to the program director about whether the training was promoting children's growth toward the important communication outcome of being able to use gestures, words, and sentences to express their wants and needs.

Future of General Outcomes Measurement for Young Children

This article describes only one application of Individual Growth and Development Indicators. Similar measures for assessing the growth of infants and toddlers are being validated in the areas of movement (Greenwood et al., in press), social development, adaptive behavior, and problem solving. Information about the reliability, validity, and practical utility of these instruments can be found in recently published articles (Greenwood et al., in press; Luze et al., 2001) and on our Web site at

The ultimate goal is to put easy-to-use assessment tools in the hands of more people working with children so that practitioners and programs will know when they are truly making a difference in moving children closer toward socially meaningful outcomes.

http://www.jgcp.ku.edu/Grants/ ecrimgd.htm. In addition, comparable sets of measures also are being developed for preschool children by the ECRI-MGD at the University of Minnesota (http://ici2.umn.edu/ecri) and for children from five to eight years at the University of Oregon (http://dibels.uoregon.edu).

The intent is to provide a sensitive, practical tool that measures growth toward important outcomes that can be used in a standardized way and that is focused on authentic child behaviors. While the measures have been constructed to meet rigorous standards of reliability and validity, a critical measure of their quality is their sensitivity to growth over time and to the effects of intervention. The ultimate goal is to put easy-to-use assessment tools in the hands of more people working with children so that practitioners and programs will know when they are truly making a difference in moving children closer toward socially meaningful outcomes.

Notes

You can reach Judith J. Carta by e-mail at carta@ukans.edu

Preparation of this manuscript was supported by Grant H024560010, funded by the Office of Special Education and Rehabilitation Services (OSERS), U. S. Department of Education Grant. The opinions expressed herein do not necessarily reflect the position or policy of the U. S. Office of Education and no official endorsement by the U. S. Office of Education should be inferred. The authors would like to thank all the team members of the ECRI-MGD project who helped conceptualize this work, and especially Gayle Luze, Deborah Linebarger, Carol Leitschuh, and Jeff Priest.

References

Centers for Disease Control and Prevention, National Center for Health Statistics. (2000). *CDC Growth Charts: United States*. Atlanta, GA: Author.

Deno, S. (1997). Whether thou goest ... Perspectives on progress monitoring. In J. W. Lloyd, E. J. Kameenui, & D. Chard (Eds.), *Issues in educating students with disabilities* (pp. 77–99). Mahwah, NJ: Erlbaum.

Deno, S. (1985). Curriculum-based measurement: The emerging alternative. *Exceptional Children, 52,* 219–232.

Deno, S. L., Mirkin, P. K., & Chaing, B. (1982). Identifying valid measures of reading. *Exceptional Children, 49,* 36–45.

Early Childhood Research Institute on Measuring Growth and Development (ECRI-MGD). (1998). *Research and development of exploring solutions assessments for children between birth to age eight* (Technical Report 5). Minneapolis, MN: Author.

Fuchs, L. S., & Fuchs, D. (1986). Linking assessment to instructional intervention: An overview. *School Psychology Review, 15,* 318–323.

Greenwood, C. R. (2001, February 6). *Monitoring growth and development of infants and toddlers*. Presentation at the Pacific Coast Research Conference, LaJolla, CA.

Greenwood, C. R., Luze, G. L., Cline, G., Kuntz, S., & Leitschuh, C. (in press). Developing a general outcome measure of growth in movement in infants and toddlers. *Topics in Early Childhood Special Education*.

Kaminski, R. A., & Good, R. H. (1996). Toward a technology for assessing basic early literacy skills. *School Psychology Review, 25,* 215–227.

Luze, G. J., Linebarger, D. L., Greenwood, C. R., Carta, J. J., Walker, D., Leitschuh, C., & Atwater, J. B. (2001). Developing a general outcome measure of growth in expressive communication of infants and toddlers. *School Psychology Review, 30,* 383–406.

McConnell, S. R., Priest, J. S., Davis, S. D., & McEvoy, M. A. (2001). Best practices in measuring growth and development for preschool children. In A. Thomas & J. Grimes (Eds.), *Best practices in school psychology IV: Vol. 2* (pp. 1231–1246). Bethesda, MD: National Association of School Psychologists (NASP).

Meisels, S. J., & Atkins-Burnett, S. (2001). The elements of early childhood assessment. In J. P. Shonkoff & S. J. Meisels (Eds.), *Handbook of early intervention* (2nd ed.) (pp. 231–257). Cambridge, UK: Cambridge University Press.

Priest, J. S., McConnell, S. R., Walker, D., Carta, J. J., Kaminski, R. A., McEvoy, M. A., Good, R. H., Greenwood, C. R., & Shinn, M. R. (in press). General growth outcomes for children between birth and age eight: Developing and validating a foundation for a continuous progress measurement system. *Journal of Early Intervention.*

Shinn, M. R. (Ed.). (1989). *Curriculum-based measurement: Assessing special children.* New York: Guilford.

Assessment for Program Planning

Creating Individualized Learning Profiles (ILP) for Young Children With Multiple, Intensive Special Needs

Kimberly A. Christensen, M.Ed., Bowling Green State University
Colleen J. Mandell, Ed.D., Bowling Green State University
Alicia B. Davis, Ph.D., University of Georgia

Bryce is a four-year, ten-month old boy who had a near-drowning accident at 18 months of age. He uses a tracheostomy tube for respiration and a gastrostomy tube to receive nourishment. Bryce has a severe seizure disorder, and cortical vision and hearing impairments, which means his eyes and ears are healthy, but the brain does not process the information effectively. His motor function is impacted by hypertonicity (high muscle tone marked by stiffness). Bryce is nonverbal, and is often unresponsive or agitated. He cannot sit unassisted and requires head support to remain in an upright position. Bryce functions at a one- to three-month developmental level across all domains, and is dependent on others for all of his daily care.

Nicholas is a two-year, nine-month old boy born with microcephaly, which is characterized by a small head size. He has been diagnosed with cerebral palsy and a seizure disorder. His vision is affected by underdeveloped optic nerves due to cerebral hemorrhages. Nicholas has chronic ear infections that impact his hearing; however, he has not been diagnosed with a permanent hearing loss. He is nonverbal and, although he can swallow, he does not have chewing capabilities. Nicholas cannot sit without support, and depends on caregivers for all of his needs. He functions at a one- to three-month developmental level across all domains.

These two vignettes describe the medical diagnoses and highlight the areas of deficit for two young children with multiple, intensive special needs. While clearly accurate, the descriptions are deficit-based and do not provide information about the children's unique strengths, preferences, or styles of learning and interacting. Too often, this is the type of diagnostic assessment information practitioners are confronted with when they begin to plan for programming. Young children with intensive special needs, like Bryce and Nicholas, present a challenge to practitioners responsible for planning and implementing intervention programs. This population of young children has multiple special needs that may include sensory, cognitive, communication, motor, social-emotional, and health care issues, which significantly impact their ability to respond to activities and experiences around them. Children with intensive special needs often display atypical responses to sound, sight, touch, and other stimuli. They may engage in self-stimulatory behavior. Some children have limited purposeful movements and responses, making it difficult to determine what motivates them. The role of the practitioner is to conduct thorough and ongoing appropriate assessments that will facilitate the development of intervention plans for young children with multiple, intensive special needs. Yet, too often, traditional assessment techniques do not provide practitioners with the quality data necessary to develop appropriate, individualized intervention plans.

Limitations of Traditional Assessment

Most standardized, norm-referenced instruments are inappropriate for assessing young children with special needs (Bagnato, Neisworth, & Munson, 1997; Linder, 1993; Sandall, McLean, & Smith, 2000). Tools

of this nature are designed to measure what a child can and cannot do in relation to a group of same-age peers. While often necessary to determine eligibility, such instruments do not indicate how a child learns. Additionally, data derived from traditional methods of assessment are static measures of a child's performance at one isolated mo-ment in time and may not represent cumulative efforts or reflect behaviors in other environments under different conditions. Criterion-referenced and norm-referenced assessment tools may not

... children with multiple, intensive special needs are often labeled "untestable" because professionals have limited experience in conducting appropriate assessments to determine their competencies ...

detect the small increments of growth that are common in children with multiple, intensive special needs (Linder, 1993). Traditional assessments often use a deficit-based model that focuses on identifying disabilities, rather than abilities. Such assessment methods rarely measure factors that are associated with a child's success, such as style of learning and interacting, level of alertness, or repertoire of physical response behaviors. Yet, if such factors are not addressed, it is impossible to conduct appropriate assessments for program planning. Thus, children with multiple, intensive special needs are often labeled "untestable" because professionals have limited experience in conducting appropriate assessments to determine their competencies (Linder, 1993).

An Alternative Model of Assessment

The Individualized Learning Profile (ILP) is an alternative approach to assessment that outlines a process for collecting information for program planning (Christensen & Mandell, 2001b). The ILP model is strengths-based and recognizes that young children with multiple, intensive special needs have the capacity to learn (Christensen & Mandell, 2001a). Like all children, they are unique, displaying individual strengths, needs, and preferences. In order to help them realize their potential for growth and development, practitioners must understand each child's individual learning style. This includes not only

... Young children with multiple, intensive special needs have the capacity to learn ... Like all children, they are unique, displaying individual strengths, needs, and preferences.

information about developmental abilities, but also how the child learns and interacts within the environment. Thus, a child's learning competencies are best measured and understood in the context of natural interactions with familiar caregivers in play settings or daily routines (Sandall et al., 2000). This article focuses on two critical aspects of the ILP model: (1) the three methods to gather assessment information, and (2) the five types of information to be gathered.

Methods to Gather Information for the ILP

The ILP utilizes three methods to gather comprehensive assessment information for program planning: (1) structured and informal systematic observations, (2) direct interactions with the child, and (3) interviews with caregivers.

Structured and Informal Systematic Observations

Assessment procedures that support an ecological perspective gather information about the child's skills and competencies within the context of natural interactions, everyday routines, and familiar settings (Bagnato et al., 1997). Documentation systems for systematic observations can range from a narrative description of the child and events taking place, to a more defined checklist that addresses specific competencies demonstrated by the child within naturally occurring activities and events (Noonan & McCormick, 1993). Structured and informal systematic observations also promote an ecological approach when practitioners assess the child's physical and social environments to determine what opportunities are available for the child to interact with or impact his or her world (Mar & Sall, 1999).

> *The ILP utilizes three methods to gather comprehensive assessment information for program planning ...*

Direct Interactions With the Child

Direct one-to-one interactions are structured opportunities for a practitioner to engage directly with a child (Mar & Sall, 1999). Gathering assessment information through direct interactions best occurs during routine activities and natural, play-based settings (Sandall et al., 2000). By following the child's cues and imitating the child's responses, the practitioner obtains a sample of the child's functional behavior (Linder, 1993). Direct one-to-one interactions allow the practitioner to elicit particular responses that a child might not demonstrate spontaneously, as well as set up opportunities for the child that encourage advanced play behaviors. Additionally, direct interactions enable the practitioner to assess characteristics such as muscle tone, as well as functional vision and hearing capacities, such as eye tracking and localizing to sound.

Interviews With Caregivers

Interviews with caregivers provide practitioners with information about the child's daily schedule; areas of strength and need; preferences for events, activities, toys, or objects; and what responses the child uses to indicate likes and dislikes (Klein, Chen, & Haney, 2000). Interviews may consist of asking significant caregivers to respond to a checklist or structured list of questions, or the practitioner may engage the caregiver in an open-ended and informal conversation (Noonan & McCormick, 1993). An additional advantage of using interviews to collect assessment information is the opportunity to promote a collaborative relationship between practitioners and caregivers.

Gathering Information for the ILP

The three methods described identify how to gather assessment information when developing an ILP for a young child with multiple, intensive special needs. What follows is a discussion of the five categories of information to be gathered: (1) biobehavioral states of arousal, (2) present levels of functioning, (3) preferences and reinforcers, (4) response behaviors, and (5) physical and social environments (see Table 1). The information in each category is based on research and recommended practice in the field of early intervention/early childhood special education. Some categories contain information that may be less familiar to practitioners. Therefore, examples with Bryce and Nicholas are interspersed throughout this article to illustrate more unfamiliar concepts. While the five categories are listed separately for discussion purposes, the essential components of the underlying processes involved in learning should not be considered in isolation; rather, they are interrelated and interdependent.

Table 1: Gathering Information for the Individualized Learning Profile

Category 1: Biobehavioral States of Arousal
Category 2: Present Levels of Functioning
Category 3: Preferences and Reinforcers
Category 4: Response Behaviors
Category 5: Physical and Social Environments

Information Gathering Category 1: Biobehavioral States of Arousal

State behavior refers to categories of arousal controlled by the central nervous system that reflect levels of alertness and attention ranging from deeply asleep to crying and/or agitated (Brazelton, 1984; Guess et al., 1988; Guess, Seigel-Causey, Roberts, Guy, & Rues, 1993). A quiet alert or active alert state is the optimum arousal level for attending to outside stimuli and learning new information (Blaha, Shafer, Smith, & Moss, 1998). A typical nervous system will allow an individual to shift between states throughout the day as appropriate for the task at hand. Children with multiple, intensive special needs may have difficulty establishing and maintaining an alert biobehavioral arousal state. They, therefore, spend a disproportionate amount of time in a drowsy or agitated state that may limit their ability to interact with their environment in meaningful ways. Health concerns, medications, and vision and/or hearing loss may all impact a child's ability to establish or maintain an

There are tools and procedures available that are appropriate to assess the arousal state of a child with multiple, intensive special needs ...

alert arousal state. There are tools and procedures available that are appropriate to assess the arousal state of a child with multiple, intensive special needs (e.g., Blaha et al., 1998; Guy, Ault, & Guess, 1993; Simeonsson, Huntington, Short, & Ware, 1988). Next, several factors to understand about biobehavioral states of arousal when developing a child's Individualized Learning Profile are illustrated. Let's consider Bryce.

Assessing Current Levels of Attending. Bryce has difficulty establishing and maintaining an alert biobehavioral state of arousal. He requires time to process information and is easily overstimulated by competing stimuli in the environment. He fluctuates between sensory overload and low arousal. Learning takes place for Bryce when he is alert and able to attend. Therefore, assessment procedures should assist the practitioner in determining Bryce's current level of attending. When identifying his current level of attending, it is important to document environmental factors such as location, time of day, his position, activity taking place, and conditions of the surroundings.

Assessing State Modulation: Internal and External Factors. Bryce's ability to modulate his state is impacted by both internal and external factors. For example, internal conditions that affect Bryce include medications prescribed for chronic pulmonary, gastrological, and neurological concerns. Additionally, Bryce is slow to become alert in the morning and is most responsive and better able to modulate his own state in the afternoon. External factors may also impact Bryce's ability to shift and maintain his biobehavioral state. When external auditory and visual stimuli overload his central nervous system, Bryce indicates his increasing level of agitation by facial grimaces, frenetic arm movements, and vocal complaints. Quiet, one-to-one interactions and the reduction of competing auditory, visual, and tactile stimuli are particularly effective in maximizing Bryce's ability to regulate and attend. Bryce's relaxed body activity and focused facial expression are physical responses that indicate he is able to shift his state to attending when extraneous conversation is eliminated, allowing communication and interactions to be directed exclusively to him.

Assessing State Modulation: Understanding the Orienting Response. Assessment procedures identify strategies and environmental adaptations that will assist Bryce in achieving and maintaining an alert, attentive state for learning. The trigger to activating an attentive state is the orienting response. The orienting response is a subconscious reflex that all human beings have that stimulates an individual to pay attention (Nelson, Johnston, & McDonnell, 2000). When an orienting response is triggered, it causes a shift in attention from either a low arousal or an agitated state to an alert state. An orienting response can be elicited by stimuli that are tolerable or pleasant and reinforcing to the individual. To avoid provoking a defensive startle, stimuli that are aversive should not be used. An orienting response can be elicited in Bryce by a change in position or by using activities, objects, voices, or sounds that he enjoys. For example, a familiar activity and his mother's voice frequently elicit an orienting response in Bryce. His smile and other physiological changes, such as eye widening, are indicators that Bryce has shifted to an alert state and is anticipating a favorite activity. Once practitioners understand how to elicit an orienting response in Bryce, these strategies can be embedded in his individualized intervention plan to assist in establishing and extending Bryce's ability to attend.

Information Gathering Category 2: Present Levels of Functioning

A collaborative assessment process allows the practitioner, in partnership with the family and other professionals, to collect information necessary for developing effective interventions (Sandall et al., 2000). Children with intensive disabilities often have multiple special needs requiring the involvement of an array of service providers to identify their strengths, abilities, and needs. Each specialist holds a piece of the puzzle that contributes to identifying how the child learns and functions within the context of his or her environment. Therefore, information about skills will often be obtained from assessments conducted by many specialists. However, the practitioner should observe and participate in the assessment process, as well as

> *A collaborative assessment process allows the practitioner, in partnership with the family and other professionals, to collect information necessary for developing effective interventions ....*

consult and communicate regularly with related service providers (Linder, 1993). Additionally, because practitioners have a major role in planning, implementing, integrating, and evaluating intervention programs, they must possess a basic knowledge across domains of developmental theories, terminology, assessments, and intervention strategies

(Sandall et al., 2000). Family members also have an integral role on the assessment team, providing direction for appropriate, individualized assessment strategies, as well as eliciting interactions with their child to demonstrate developmental abilities. There are tools and procedures available that are appropriate to assess present levels of functioning for children with multiple, intensive special needs (e.g., Morgan & Watkins, 1989; Stillman, 1974), as well as resources that provide a more thorough discussion of specific assessment instruments (e.g., Bagnato et al., 1997; Mar & Cerruto, 2000).

Following are factors to understand about present levels of functioning when developing a child's ILP. When determining present levels of functioning, the key developmental domains to assess include: sensorimotor, communication, cognition, and social development. Each developmental domain is interrelated and cannot be assessed in isolation. There are several additional factors about a child that the team should consider when developing the present levels of functioning category on the ILP. These include the child's diagnosis; medical concerns; areas of strength and need; emerging skills; functional hearing and vision capacities; and ways in which the child's disability impacts growth, development, and learning. Determining present levels of functioning for an ILP is important because it generates a "snapshot" of a child's functional repertoire of existing skills.

Information Gathering Category 3: Preferences and Reinforcers

Stimuli, events, or activities that an individual enjoys are preferences. Understanding and identifying individual preferences allows the practitioner to embed experiences the child enjoys within programming to reinforce and motivate interest in an activity or lesson (Mason & Egel, 1995). When an individual perceives a learning experience as meaningful or pleasurable, his or her interest and participation are increased. It often is difficult to determine what is motivating to young children with multiple, intensive special needs who may be limited in their ability to respond to materials, activities, and experiences around them. Yet, when practitioners are able to effectively interpret responses and identify a child's likes and dislikes, these preferences will serve as powerful, motivating reinforcers. Appropriate tools and procedures are available to assess the likes and dislikes of a child with multiple, intensive special needs (e.g., Klein et al., 2000; Korsten, Dunn, Foss, & Francke, 1993; Mason & Egel, 1995).

Two strategies for determining individual preferences include gathering information from caregivers and conducting systematic, ongoing reinforcer assessments. Information about a child's likes and dislikes should be collected from all significant caregivers, either through an interview or questionnaire. Family members, child care providers, and other significant caregivers provide valuable information about the child's interests based on their knowledge of him or her within the context of daily routines (Klein et al., 2000).

The second method for collecting reliable information about a child's preferences is through systematic, ongoing reinforcer assessments. Often practitioners make assumptions about what they believe might be reinforcing to a child, without assessing for preferences systematically (Green, Reid, White, Halford, Brittain, & Gardner, 1988). Additionally, a child's preferences may change frequently throughout the day due to any number of factors, including satiation or boredom with the material or activity (Mason, McGee, Farmer-Dougan, & Risley, 1989). Therefore, even after the initial reinforcer assessment is completed, the practitioner should conduct regular, frequent assessment probes before implementing intervention plans (Gast, Jacobs, Logan, & Murray, 2000). For

Often practitioners make assumptions about what they believe might be reinforcing to a child, without assessing for preferences systematically ...

example, the practitioner or caregiver can present a variety of familiar and novel sensory materials and toys to determine a child's preferences prior to instruction.

Identifying and understanding the child's likes and dislikes will assist the practitioner in determining the child's preferred sensory modality (Korsten et al., 1993). An individual child's responses when engaging in activities and natural behaviors provide a profile of preferred sensory stimuli. Preferences should be assessed across auditory, visual, tactile, olfactory, gustatory, and social modalities (Mason & Egel, 1995). Additionally, sensory modalities such as vestibular, which is related to balance; proprioception, which involves movement and spatial orientation; and kinesthetic, which refers to body position, weight, and movement must also be considered (Blaha et al., 1998). Once a preferred list of sensory modalities has been identified, activities that provide sensory input from that modality should be included in the child's intervention program to increase motivation and provide reinforcement (Korsten et al., 1993).

Information Gathering Category 4: Response Behaviors

Response behaviors refer to the repertoire of reactions an individual demonstrates, either intentionally or reflexively, when exposed to stimuli

(Korsten et al., 1993). Responses can be neutral, positive, or negative and are indicated by behaviors such as movement, vocalization, and affect. Preferences and aversions are often communicated by the way an individual responds to activities, experiences, or events. Understanding a child's likes and dislikes by accurately interpreting his or her behavioral responses allows the practitioner or caregiver to recognize and respect communicative intent and design motivating intervention plans. Additionally, identifying and interpreting behavioral responses enhances the assessment of a child's functional strengths and abilities. For example, by determining a child's individual repertoire of response behaviors, the practitioner will more clearly understand how the child demonstrates skills and competencies.

Interpreting the response behaviors of young children with multiple, intensive disabilities is challenging. Yet all human beings, regardless of the extent of their special needs, demonstrate response behaviors. Even the child who appears unresponsive may react to stimuli by exhibiting physiological responses such as a gag reflex, startle, yawn, or change in pulse rate and respiration. By conducting systematic assessments to identify and interpret response behaviors, the practitioner begins to understand the signals a child uses, often unintentionally, to communicate wants and needs and to indicate functional abilities (Korsten et al., 1993). There are tools and procedures available that are appropriate to assess the response behaviors of a child with multiple, intensive special needs (e.g., Blaha et al., 1998; Guy et al., 1993; Klein et al., 2000; Korsten et al., 1993). Following are several factors to understand about interpreting response behaviors when developing a child's ILP. Let's consider Nicholas as we address each of these factors.

Assessing Random/Reflexive Response Behaviors. Identifying and interpreting Nicholas' response behaviors begins with the practitioner observing his physical reactions to stimuli, activities, and interactions. Some of Nicholas' responses are reflexive, such as his reaction to bright light. When a light box is turned on and off, he reflexively opens and closes his eyes and mouth. Nicholas also exhibits a strong startle reflex to sound. Random and reflexive behavior can be shaped into intentional responses to facilitate communication and functional skill development. For example, the practitioner capitalizes on Nicholas' reflexive grasp, using it as a mechanism for integrating his visual and motor systems by wrapping the long colorful streamers of a wand around his hand and then moving the wand slowly within his visual field.

Assessing Purposeful Response Behaviors. In order to identify Nicholas' repertoire of physical response behaviors, the practitioner should systematically assess his random and purposeful reactions to stimuli, activities, and interactions. Nicholas most often demonstrates response behaviors by a change in affect, eye gaze, movement, and vocalization. For example, Nicholas responds to a visual stimulus by shifting his eye gaze, stiffening his body, smiling, laughing, and vocalizing. Nicholas demonstrates consistent intentional response behaviors to stimuli he perceives as aversive or pleasurable. When overstimulated, upset, or uncomfortable, he grimaces, cries, and exhibits increased muscle tone. On the other hand, he smiles, laughs, and vocalizes to indicate enjoyment.

Assessing Physical Response Behaviors. When systematically testing for response behaviors, it is critical that Nicholas' voluntary and involuntary movements are assessed when he is in a variety of positions. Questions to consider include:

- What conditions support his performance and expansion of functional skills?
- What can he do by himself?
- What does he need help doing?

Nicholas' physical response behaviors also are indicators of his functional strengths and abilities. For example, with direction from the vision specialist, the practitioner assesses Nicholas' functional vision by identifying his reactions to a visual stimulus, studying his responses to determine if he sees light when a flashlight is held in front of him. Questions to consider include:

- What response behaviors does Nicholas exhibit?
- Does he blink his eyes or stare?
- Do his body movements become still or is he agitated?

The practitioner also assesses his visual field by moving the flashlight in different locations to determine where he sees best, noting the physical position he is in when he indicates a response. By assessing Nicholas' response behaviors, the practitioner can identify the repertoire of signals he uses, either intentionally or reflexively, to communicate his wants and needs and indicate his functional abilities.

Information Gathering Category 5: Physical and Social Environments

Assessment practices should identify how the young child interacts with his or her world. The most effective assessment of the child's competencies occurs in the context of natural interactions with familiar caregivers (Sandall et al., 2000). Therefore, it is critical that assessment procedures consider the child's physical and social environments. Young children learn best when they experience responsive physical environments as well as positive, supportive social interactions. Developmentally appropriate intervention practices provide young children opportunities to make choices, develop independence, and interact

Assessment practices should identify how the young child interacts with his or her world.

with their environments in meaningful ways (Bredekamp & Copple, 1997). However, the growth and development of children with intensive special needs is often compromised due to limited opportunities for independent learning and play. This population of children depends on caregivers to interpret the meaning of their responses, identify what motivates them, and provide them with opportunities for engaging in independent play. Additionally, responsive social interactions are often restricted by the challenge of interpreting the child's cues. There are tools and procedures with components that provide information about the opportunities for interaction within a child's physical and social environments (e.g., Guy et al., 1993; Klein et al., 2000; Mar & Sall, 1999).

Following are factors to consider about physical and social environments when developing a child's ILP.

Assessing Physical Environments. Assessment procedures begin by identifying what opportunities are available for the child to interact with or impact his or her world. When children have limited ability to interact independently, they depend on caregivers to provide opportunities that allow them to experience a physical environment that is responsive and controllable. Thus, when assessing young children with multiple, intensive special needs, the practitioner should consider not only what the child is able to do, but also what the environment is able to provide. Some questions to consider are:

- Does the child have opportunities to engage in independent play?
- Are materials, activities, and experiences selected based on the child's preferences?
- Are surroundings and experiences accessible given the individual child's physical ability to interact?
- Are environmental conditions such as noise level, temperature of the room, and natural and artificial light conducive to the child's learning and arousal style?

Assessing Social Environments. The social environment includes opportunities available for the child and significant caregivers and peers to engage in reciprocal interactions. Early communication for young children with multiple, intensive special needs begins with establishing nurturing, responsive relationships that are characterized by activities such as consoling, bonding, interpreting cues, and turn-taking games (Klein et al., 2000). Some questions to consider when assessing the social environment include:

- Are caregivers able to consistently interpret the meaning of the child's responses?
- Does the child have frequent opportunities for meaningful one-to-one interactions that focus on social reciprocity (e.g., turn-taking games)?
- Do caregivers recognize and respond to the communicative functions of the child's behavior?

Consideration of the physical and social environments for a child's ILP underscores that learning occurs as a result of responsive interactions between a child and his or her environment.

Outlining the ILP Process

The ILP process begins when the team assembles to collaborate in planning and implementing assessment for program planning. At this time, decisions are made about the instruments and strategies that will be used

Table 2: Resource List of Tools and Procedures to Assess Learning
Competencies

Category 1: Biobehavioral States of Arousal

Title: *Thoughts on the Assessment of the Student With the Most Profound Disabilities*
Author(s): R. Blaha, S. Shafer, M. Smith, & K. Moss

Title: *Project ABLE Manual: Analyzing Behavior State and Learning Environments*
Author(s): B. Guy, M. Ault, & D. Guess

Title: *Carolina Record of Individual Behavior (CRIB)*
Author(s): R. J. Simeonsson, G. S. Huntington, R. J. Short, & W. B. Ware

Category 2: Present Levels of Functioning

Title: *Assessment of Developmental Skills for Young Multihandicapped Sensory
Impaired Children: An Instructional Manual for the INSITE Developmental Checklist*
Author(s): E. Morgan & S. Watkins (Eds.)

Title: *Callier-Azusa Scale (CAS): Assessment of Deaf-Blind Children*
Author(s): R. Stillman

Title: *Linking Assessment and Early Intervention: An Authentic Curriculum-Based
Approach*
Author(s): S. J. Bagnato, J. T. Neisworth, & S. M. Munson

Title: *Psychoeducational Assessment of Students Who Have Severe, Multiple
Disabilities Including Deafblindness*
Author(s): H. H. Mar & A. Cerruto

Category 3: Preferences and Reinforcers

Title: *Promoting Learning Through Active Interaction: A Guide to Early
Communication With Young Children Who Have Multiple Disabilities*
Author(s): M. D. Klein, D. Chen, & M. Haney

Title: *Every Move Counts: Sensory-Based Communication Techniques*
Author(s): J. E. Korsten, D. K. Dunn, T. V. Foss, & M. K. Francke

Title: *What Does Amy Like? Using a Mini-Reinforcer Assessment to Increase Student
Participation in Instructional Activities*
Author(s): S. A. Mason & A. L. Egel

Category 4: Response Behaviors

Title: *Thoughts on the Assessment of the Studnet With the Most Profound Disabilities*
Author(s): R. Blaha, S. Shafer, M. Smith, & K. Moss

Title: *Project ABLE Manual: Analyzing Behavior State and Learning Environments
Profile*
Author(s): B. Guy, M. Ault, & D. Guess

Table 2: Continued

Title: *Promoting Learning Through Active Interaction: A Guide to Early Communication With Young Children Who Have Multiple Disabilities*
Author(s): M. D. Klein, D. Chen, & M. Haney

Title: *Every Move Counts: Sensory-Based Communication Techniques*
Author(s): J. E. Korsten, D. K. Dunn, T. V. Foss, & M. K. Francke

Category 5: Physical and Social Environments

Title: *Project ABLE Manual: Analyzing Behavior State and Learning Environments Profile*
Author(s): B. Guy, M. Ault, & D. Guess

Title: *Promoting Learning Through Active Interaction: A Guide to Early Communication With Young Children Who Have Multiple Disabilities*
Author(s): M. D. Klein, D. Chen, & M. Haney

Title: *Dimensions of Communication: An Instrument to Assess the Communication Skills and Behaviors of Individuals With Disabilities*
Author(s): H. H. Mar & N. Sall

Note: Consult the References of this article for publishing information about the tools and procedures identified in Table 2.

to assess learning competencies. The ILP model identifies parameters for gathering information about the underlying processes involved in learning by collecting assessment data in five categories: (1) biobehavioral states of arousal, (2) present levels of functioning, (3) preferences and reinforcers, (4) response behaviors, and (5) physical and social environments. Within each of the five categories, discussed previously, is a suggested list of assessment tools and procedures that teams may select (see Table 2). While this list is not exhaustive, the resources identified are appropriate for assessing young children with multiple, intensive special needs.

As teams become more familiar with the types of information to be collected, they can design informal tools and data collection forms to supplement the formal instruments. When the assessment process is complete, an individualized profile of a child's competencies will emerge. The team shares and discusses assessment results, and from this information an interrelated, strengths-based report is written. The report not only addresses functional skills and developmental abilities, but also identifies and discusses the implications of the child's level of alertness, preferences, physical response behaviors, and style of learning and interacting.

Additionally, the team considers how the physical and social environments can support the child's learning and development.

Using the comprehensive assessment information generated by the ILP, the team plans program goals, objectives, and activities that provide opportunities for independent play, direct systematic instruction, and embedded learning opportunities. The ILP is a fluid, ongoing process that continues after the initial program plan is determined. Recognizing that assessment is linked to programming, the team must monitor progress on an ongoing basis to evaluate the effectiveness of interventions and modify the program as needed. A continuous assessment process recognizes that young children with multiple, intensive special needs, like all children, demonstrate changes in health, growth, and development. The following vignette shares information from Bryce's ILP that describes his learning style and competencies, and highlights one activity from his program plan. This strengths-based philosophy, rather than a traditional deficit or fix-it approach, identifies assessment information that can be used to design activities that build on Bryce's competencies.

This strengths-based philosophy, rather than a traditional deficit or fix-it approach, identifies assessment information that can be used to design activities that build on Bryce's competencies.

Bryce has many strengths, which include vocal turn taking and showing emotions, such as smiling, laughing, and crying at appropriate times. He expresses discomfort, protest, and pleasure through vocalizations, facial expressions, and increased arm movements. Bryce is very social and enjoys engaging in physical contact activities like roughhousing and cuddling. He alerts to auditory stimuli, especially familiar voices, music, and environmental sounds. Although Bryce prefers auditory stimuli, he is able to use his vision to track an object within 14 inches of his personal space. He can randomly wave his arms in a wide, out-stretched arc when lying in a supported position on his back.

Bryce's caregivers and practitioner understand that his 14-inch visual field and random ability to move his arms are strengths. In order to address a program goal that focuses on cause and effect, they collaborate to create a play surface with sound resonating qualities on which Bryce can lie. Suspended 14 inches above him on a bar are objects and toys. All of the items selected are based on Bryce's preferences for music and sound and his ability to interact with the objects using random arm movements. When Bryce's arms come into contact with an object, the resultant sound or music rewards his actions. He alerts by becoming very still and listens intently for several seconds as he processes the sound, and then smiles widely. Several seconds after the sound or music ends, he begins to wave his arms again. As a result, Bryce experiences an independent opportunity for play in an environment that is responsive and controllable.

Conclusion

The ILP model provides a rationale and outlines a process for practitioners and teams to plan and implement initial and ongoing assessments for program planning for young children with multiple, intensive special needs. Strengths-based information about the child's learning style and competencies is generated by gathering assessment data in five categories: (1) biobehavioral states of arousal, (2) present levels of functioning, (3) preferences and reinforcers, (4) response behaviors, and (5) physical and social environments. Use of the ILP assessment model directs the team in identifying not only goals and objectives, but also activities that are useful to create opportunities for independent play, provide direct systematic instruction, and embed learning opportunities within daily routines. With appropriate programming, young children with multiple, intensive special needs can realize their potential as independent, active learners.

Notes

You can reach Kimberly A. Christensen by e-mail at kchris@bgnet.bgsu.edu

The activities described in this article were partially supported by Grant #H029A70142 and Grant #H325A990084 from the Office of Special Education Programs, U.S. Department of Education.

References

Bagnato, S. J., Neisworth, J. T., & Munson, S. M. (1997). *Linking assessment and early intervention: An authentic curriculum-based approach*. Baltimore: Paul H. Brookes.

Blaha, R., Shafer, S., Smith, M., & Moss, K. (1998). Thoughts on the assessment of the student with the most profound disabilities. In Texas School for the Blind and Visually Impaired Outreach Program (Ed.), *Students with profound impairments: Gathering information and planning instruction* (pp. 2–10) [Information packet]. Austin, TX: Texas School for the Blind and Visually Impaired Outreach Program.

Brazelton, T. B. (1984). *Neonatal behavioral assessment scale* (2nd ed.). Philadelphia, PA: Lippincott, Spastics International Medical Publications.

Bredekamp, S., & Copple, C. (Eds.). (1997). *Developmentally appropriate practice in early childhood programs* (Rev. ed.). Washington, DC: National Association for the Education of Young Children (NAEYC).

Christensen, K. A., & Mandell, C. J. (2001a). *Volume I: An introduction to enhancing the assessment of infants, toddlers, and young children with intensive special needs* [Videotape]. Bowling Green, OH: Bowling Green State University, Division of Intervention Services.

Christensen, K. A., & Mandell, C. J. (2001b). *Volume II: The ENHANCE model of assessment for infants, toddlers, and young children with intensive special needs* [Videotape]. Bowling Green, OH: Bowling Green State University, Division of Intervention Services.

Gast, D. L., Jacobs, H. A., Logan, K. R., & Murray, A. S. (2000). Pre-session assessment of preferences for students with profound multiple disabilities. *Education and Training in Mental Retardation and Developmental Disabilities, 35*, 393–405.

Green, C. W., Reid, D. H., White, L. K., Halford, R. C., Brittain, D. P., & Gardner, S. M. (1988). Identifying reinforcers for persons with profound handicaps: Staff opinion versus systematic assessment of preferences. *Journal of Applied Behavior Analysis, 21*, 31–43.

Guess, D., Mulligan-Ault, M., Roberts, S., Struth, J., Siegal-Causey, E., Thompson, B., Bronicki, G. J., & Guy, B. (1988). Implications of biobehavioral states for the education and treatment of students with the most handicapping conditions. *Journal of the Association for Persons With Severe Handicaps, 13,* 163–174.

Guess, D., Siegal-Causey, E., Roberts, S., Guy, B., & Rues, J. (1993). Analysis of state organizational patterns among students with profound disabilities. *Journal of the Association for Persons With Severe Handicaps, 18,* 93–108.

Guy, B., Ault, M., & Guess, D. (1993). *Project ABLE manual: Analyzing behavior state and learning environments profile.* Lawrence, KS: University of Kansas, Department of Special Education.

Klein, M. D., Chen, D., & Haney, M. (2000). *Promoting learning through active interaction: A guide to early communication with young children who have multiple disabilities.* Baltimore: Paul H. Brookes.

Korsten, J. E., Dunn, D. K., Foss, T. V., & Francke, M. K. (1993). *Every move counts: Sensory-based communication techniques.* San Antonio, TX: Therapy Skill Builders.

Linder, T. W. (1993). *Transdisciplinary play-based assessment* (Rev. ed.). Baltimore: Paul H. Brookes.

Mar, H. H., & Cerruto, A. (2000). *Psychoeducational assessment of students who have severe, multiple disabilities including deafblindness: Assessment tools manual.* Unpublished manuscript, St Luke's Roosevelt Hospital Center.

Mar, H. H., & Sall, N. (1999). *Dimensions of communication: An instrument to assess the communication skills and behaviors of individuals with disabilities.* New York: St. Luke's Roosevelt Hospital Center.

Mason, S. A., & Egel, A. L. (1995). What does Amy like? Using a mini-reinforcer assessment to increase student participation in instructional activities. *Teaching Exceptional Children, 28*(1), 42–45.

Mason, S. A., McGee, G. G., Farmer-Dougan, V., & Risley, T. R. (1989). A practical strategy for ongoing reinforcer assessment. *Journal of Applied Behavior Analysis, 22*(2), 171–179.

Morgan, E., & Watkins, S. (Eds.). (1989). *Assessment of developmental skills for young multihandicapped sensory impaired children: An instruction manual for the INSITE developmental checklist.* Logan, UT: Hope, Inc.

Nelson, C., Johnston, S., & McDonnell, A. (2000, December 9). *Getting to know you—Child-guided strategies for understanding children with severe disabilities: The van Dijk approach to assessment.* Paper presented at the DEC International Early Childhood Conference on Children With Special Needs, Albuquerque, NM.

Noonan, M. J., & McCormick, L. (1993). *Early intervention in natural environments: Methods and procedures.* Belmont, CA: Brooks/Cole.

Sandall, S., McLean, M. E., & Smith, B. J. (2000). *DEC recommended practices in early intervention/early childhood special education.* Longmont, CO: Sopris West.

Simeonsson, R. J., Huntington, G. S., Short, R. J., & Ware, W. B. (1988). *The Carolina record of individual behavior (CRIB): Characteristics of handicapped infants and children.* Chapel Hill, NC: Frank Porter Graham Child Development Center, University of North Carolina at Chapel Hill.

Stillman, R. (1974). *Callier-Azusa scale (CAS): Assessment of deaf-blind children.* Reston, VA: Council for Exceptional Children (CEC).

Ecological Assessment and Planning

Linda McCormick, Ph.D., University of Hawaii
Mary Jo Noonan, Ph.D., University of Hawaii

Planning Decisions

Of all the assessment decisions necessary for identifying and serving young children with disabilities, the decisions related to planning interventions are in many ways the most important and the most challenging. The critical intervention decisions are:

1. What are intervention goals and objectives?
2. Where should intervention be provided?
3. How should intervention be provided?
4. When should intervention be provided?
5. How can we continuously evaluate intervention?

The theoretical framework best suited to answering these questions and guiding the planning process is ecological theory. Ecological theory had its roots in the ecological psychology tradition of Barker (1968) and Bronfenbrenner (1979). The central thesis is that behavior cannot be understood apart from its context. More specifically, Bronfenbrenner (1977) argued that the results of assessment have limited usefulness for planning unless they are referenced against the social, behavioral, and educational expectations of activities and persons in a child's natural environments. To plan for young children's participation in inclusive environments we must consider the children's behavior in relation to the demands and expectations of their unique environments. The assessment process described in this article and other articles by the first author and colleagues (McCormick & Noonan, 1996; McCormick, Wong, & Yogi, 2002) applies ecological assessment procedures in one environment—the preschool classroom. However, the same procedures can easily be applied in other natural environments (e.g., home, community, recreation/leisure).

Diagnostic assessment instruments, which are typically used to document eligibility for specialized services, compare the child's performance in relation to the normative population used to standardize the test. Traditional developmental scales identify the developmental deficits of the child whose skills are being assessed. For example, they may tell us that a three-year old child is functioning at a two-year level. More specifically we might note that the child cannot: (1) recognize six different colors, (2) name five different shapes, (3) jump forward with both feet, (4) identify means to a goal, and (5) engage in imaginary play. The problem, however, with these types of tests is that too often the results are used improperly to guide intervention. The results obtained do not tell us what children need to learn in order to participate independently in activities with their peers in their particular preschool or what they need to learn to participate in daily routines (e.g., meals, outings to the park, grocery shopping) with their own particular family.

Initially applied to developing goals and objectives for learners with severe and multiple disabilities by Brown and colleagues (1979) in the late seventies, ecological assessment is now widely suggested for use with children with all levels and types of disabilities in many environments, including inclusive preschool settings (e.g., Edmiaston, Dolezal, Doolittle, Erickson, & Merritt, 2000; Grisham-Brown & Hemmeter, 1998; Haney & Cavallaro, 1996; McCormick & Noonan, 1996). Through this process we discover what a child needs to learn, where and when to provide intervention, what adaptations and supports must be provided so the child can learn new skills, and what opportunities are available for data collection. The latter is especially important, as determining data collection procedures that are realistic for inclusive environments and suitable for functional objectives continues to be a challenge for most preschool teachers.

There are two basic steps to conducting the Ecological Assessment and Planning Process. The first is formulating goals and objectives. This requires: (1) listing daily routines and activities and general expectations for children's behavior in these daily activities and routines; (2) comparing the present skills and abilities of the child with special needs to these general expectations; and (3) devising functional goals and objectives for the individual child. The second step in the process is

Through this process we discover what a child needs to learn, where and when to provide intervention, what adaptations and supports must be provided so the child can learn new skills, and what opportunities are available for data collection.

matrix planning, which requires deciding: (1) precisely when opportunities to learn and practice the identified goals and objectives will be provided throughout the day; (2) what adaptations and supports will be provided; and (3) how progress will be monitored.

The best way to describe the Ecological Assessment and Planning Process is by example, so we will follow one child, Adam, through the process. Adam is in his first week at the Aloha Community Preschool.

Adam's Story

Because he is so small for his age, many people think that Adam is much younger than four. A congenital heart defect associated with his diagnosis of Down syndrome kept Adam in the hospital for a considerable percentage of his first four years of life. Now with the surgery behind them, his mother (a single parent) is pleased that Adam is enrolled in the same community preschool that his brother attended.

Adam's preferences are very clear. He loves music, being pushed on the swing, water and sand play, large blocks, dinosaurs, and toy cars. Equally clear is what he does not like. He does not like the slides, the climbing equipment, or the tricycles (probably because of his lack of experience and poor muscle tone and strength). Similarly, he avoids activities that require fine motor precision (e.g., using scissors and glue, puzzles with small pieces). When offered choices (e.g., toys, materials, foods, activities) Adam either grabs what he wants or just walks away. Adam uses some words but most of his communication is with gestures and facial expressions. He follows simple directions, matches some colors and shapes, and sometimes imitates peers. Adam's mother reports that at home he follows his six-year old brother around and tries to imitate everything he does. He will listen to a story being read or turn the pages and look at a picture book for a brief period of time. Adam has not learned to share or take turns. He tends to stand on the periphery of activities, watching rather than participating. For example, at center time when the teacher suggests that he join a group of children building with the large blocks, he will gather up an assortment of blocks, move them to one corner of the block area, and then sit down to play with his back to the other children in the area. While Adam still has occasional toileting accidents, he is doing well with toileting independently but needs reminders and some assistance with dressing. Adam likes most foods and feeds himself and drinks from a cup with minimum spilling.

On Thursday afternoon of Adam's first week of preschool, the team has assembled to develop appropriate learning objectives for Adam that also will reflect the developmentally appropriate curriculum (Bredekamp & Copple, 1997) used in the Aloha Community Preschool.

The team includes Selina (teacher), Lisa (educational assistant), Jessie (early childhood special education teacher consultant), Sung Lee (speech-language pathologist), and Kelly (Adam's mother). Jonathan (occupational therapist) was not able to attend this meeting. Kelly, Adam's mother, is an especially important member of the team. She will have a major voice in describing Adam's present abilities and identifying the skills that will be targeted for instruction and practice.

Adam is the first child with a disability to be included in this classroom. Jessie, Sung Lee, and Jonathan will visit the classroom weekly to consult with Selina and Lisa and to observe and work with Adam. Sometimes they will work with him individually or, more often, in small groups with his peers.

Prior to beginning the assessment and planning process, discussion focuses on the importance of ensuring that Adam's objectives:

- Align with the developmentally appropriate practices that guide the preschool's integrated curriculum;

- Can be addressed and measured within the context of daily activities and routines;

- Address his parent's concerns about self-care skills, choice making, and developing friendships and positive interpersonal relationships;

- Reflect the priorities of all team members (related service personnel as well as the parent and the teachers);

- Contribute to Adam becoming a member of the classroom community.

Thus, the team began the Ecological Assessment and Planning Process. They also identified times and dates when Adam's mother would be able to attend future team meetings to evaluate Adam's progress and revise the plan as needed. The steps in the process are described and summarized in Table 1.

Ecological Assessment and Planning Process

Step 1: List Daily Activities and Routines

To begin the process, the team creates a list of the activities and routines in the order that they occur on a typical day in the inclusive preschool classroom. Then, using the "Ecological Assessment and Planning Form" (see Figure 1), they write a title for each activity or routine in the first column where it says "Activity/Routine." Note that the example in Figure 1 shows only the first two pages of the "Ecological Assessment

Table 1: Ecological Assessment and Planning Process

Step 1: *List daily activities and routines.* List the activities and routines in the order that they occur on a typical day.

Step 2: *List major behavioral expectations.* For each activity/routine, indicate the key behaviors that children (i.e., the class as a whole) are expected to demonstrate in the activity. Certainly every child will not demonstrate every behavior on every occasion.

Step 3: *Evaluate present performance.* Consider the strengths and instructional needs of the target child in relation to the daily activities. On the assessment form, write a checkmark to indicate whether the child "can do" or "needs to learn" the behavior and note relevant observations in the "Comments" column (see Figure 1).

Step 4: *Formulate objectives.* Formulate objectives that will enable the child to participate independently in the classroom activities/routines.

Step 5: *Plan adaptations and supports.* Transfer brief statements of the objective from the "Ecological Assessment and Planning Form" to the "Adaptations, Supports, and Data Collection Form" (see Figure 2). Decide which adaptations and/or supports will enable the child to learn and practice the target behavior when opportunities present themselves. The four broad categories of adaptations and supports are: (1) scaffolding and practice, (2) adapting the task and/or modifying materials, (3) changing task expectations, and (4) arranging peer assistance.

Step 6: *Decide who will provide the adaptations and supports.* Indicate who has responsibility for assisting with and teaching each objective.

Step 7: *Plan data collection opportunities and procedures.* List the child's objectives across the horizontal axis of a matrix and daily activities on the vertical axis (see Figure 3). Record opportunities and responses or a comment about the behavior in the cells.

and Planning Form" completed for Adam. There were actually two more pages with six additional activities.

Step 2: List Major Behavioral Expectations

For each activity/routine, indicate the key behaviors that children are expected to demonstrate in the activity. For example, as shown in Figure 1, the key behaviors for the "Arrival" routine in Adam's classroom are: (1) greeting the teacher and responding to, "How are you?" (2) saying good-bye to their parent(s); (3) putting belongings in their cubby; (4) selecting and playing with a toy at a table or center; and (5) playing and sharing with peers.

Certainly every child will not demonstrate every one of these behaviors on every occasion. The point is to list broad developmentally appropriate expectations for the class as a whole. State expectations in positive terms (e.g., avoid statements like "no grabbing toys"). It is also important that expectations reflect a preference for children's active engagement. Thus, avoid or keep to a minimum expectation statements such as, "sit quietly" and "wait in line." Developmentally appropriate practice recommendations do not support idle waiting (either sitting or standing) at any time (including transition times) (Bredekamp & Copple, 1997) for young children. Neither the brain nor the body can grow without engagement.

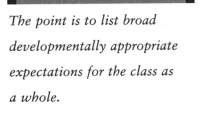

The point is to list broad developmentally appropriate expectations for the class as a whole.

Teachers who use the "Ecological Assessment and Planning Form" on a regular basis report that they have three or four different "expectation lists" that they can "plug in" depending on when they are planning. As would be assumed, their expectations for the class change considerably over the course of a school year.

Step 3: Evaluate Present Performance

The focus now shifts from the teacher's behavioral expectations for the class as a whole to the strengths and instructional needs of the focus child. Note that on the sample "Ecological Assessment and Planning Form" (Figure 1) the team observed that Adam said good-bye to his mother and put his belongings in his cubby. They agreed that Adam needed to learn to greet and respond to the teacher upon entering the room, select a toy and play with it at a table or in a center, and share toys with his peers.

Figure 1: Ecological Assessment and Planning for Adam

Ecological Assessment and Planning Form

Team Members: _Selina, Lisa, Jessie, Sung Lee, Kelly, Jonathan_   Date: _9-2-02_

Child: _Adam_

Activities/Routines and Expectations	Can Do	Needs to Learn	Comments	Objectives
Activity/Routine _Arrival_				
Greet—say "Hi" & respond to "How are you?"		✔	No response—looks at the teacher and goes inside	Will greet teacher at the door upon arrival
Say good-bye to parent	✔			
Put belongings in cubby	✔		Looks for his photo and then places his things in his cubby	
Select toy & play table or a center		✔	Just walks around the room—seems unclear about what is expected	Will select a toy or activity center at arrival time
Play/share toys with peers		✔	Only parallel play	Will play cooperatively with peers
Activity/Routine _Circle_				
Move to carpet area/sit in circle	✔		Follows the other children	
Focus visual attention on teacher	✔			
Raise hand & answer "I am here"		✔	Raises his hand but not speech	Will respond verbally (as well as raising his hand) when teacher calls the roll

Figure 1 Continued

Activity/Routine and Expectations	Can Do	Needs to Learn	Comments	Objectives
Activity/Routine Circle				
Sing/do hand motions for songs	✓		Watches and tries to imitate peers	
Answer when asked questions about the story		✓	No response	Will respond (by pointing or verbalizing) to questions about a story
Activity/Routine Art				
Request & assemble materials		✓	Didn't seem to understand about getting materials from table	Will independently retrieve art materials from the supply table
Use materials properly		✓	Difficulty cutting and squeezing glue bottle—line with crayons	Will increase cutting and gluing skills
Follow activity directions		✓	Forgets what to do after the first step of the activity	Will follow 2- and 3-step directions for art activities
Share & take turns with materials		✓	Threw scissors/glue on the floor when asked to share	Will share materials in art activities
Clean up/put away materials	✓		Imitates peers	
Activity/Routine Snack				
Wash & dry hands & throw away the paper towel	✓		Encountered some problem getting him to leave the water	
Pass plates & napkins	✓			
Find a chair and sit	✓			
Eat & drink independently	✓		Does well with a small cup—eats everything he is given	
Throw trash in container	✓			

To gather information about the child's current skills in relation to daily routines/activities, ideally the child should be observed during a week or more as he participates in the classroom activities/routines. Also, information available from other sources (e.g., his mother's observations, diagnostic tests, developmental scales) may be helpful at this point. Using all the information gathered, team members are able to present a clear picture of the child's skills and instructional needs in relation to the daily activities. As the team describes the child's current performance, they place a checkmark to indicate whether the child "can do" or "needs to learn" each behavior and note relevant observations in the "Comments" column of the "Ecological Assessment and Planning Form."

Step 4: Formulate Objectives

Now it is time to formulate objectives that will enable the child to participate independently in the classroom activities/routines. Objectives for Adam in the first activity (see Figure 1) are to greet the teacher, select a toy or activity, and play cooperatively with peers. By definition, these objectives are meaningful and functional because they facilitate engagement and participation in Adam's preschool environment. The fact that the target behaviors are embedded in daily routines means that there will be *at least one* opportunity for instruction of each target behavior each day. In most cases there will be three to five opportunities each day for practice of the targeted skills. The number of practice opportunities for each skill each day is estimated by perusing the "Objectives" column and noting that target behaviors are performed in different activities throughout the day. For example, Adam's team estimated there would be at least five opportunities per day to practice playing cooperatively with peers.

... Formulate objectives that will enable the child to participate independently in the classroom activities/routines.

Step 5: Plan Adaptations and Supports

The team then transfers brief statements of the objectives from the "Ecological Assessment and Planning Form" to the "Adaptations, Supports, and Data Collection Form." Figure 2 shows the first page of the "Adaptations, Supports, and Data Collection Form" completed for Adam. For each objective the team must decide if providing an adaptation and/or support will promote practice and, ultimately, independent performance of the behavior. Adaptations are made only when necessary, and are as unobtrusive as possible. Calling attention to adaptations or supports provided to children with special needs may stigmatize them in front of their peers. Further, providing adaptations unnecessarily can lead to the child waiting for and thus becoming dependent on assistance and prompts. The "Adaptations, Supports, and Data Collection Form" suggests four broad categories of adaptations and supports. They are:

1. *Scaffolding and practice.* Scaffolding is providing the minimum amount of assistance necessary until the child is able to perform the task independently (Vygotsky, 1978). Over time, the amount of adult assistance is gradually adjusted until it is completely withdrawn. Asking questions that promote discovery and exploration, structuring appropriately challenging but achievable opportunities for practice of new behaviors, and pausing so that the child finishes sentences in a familiar story all are forms of scaffolding.

2. *Adapting the task and/or modifying materials.* Some ways that tasks may be adapted are shortening the task, simplifying the directions, providing visual directions, and/or reducing the number of steps. Materials can be modified by changing their size and/or other dimensions; attaching suction cups, clamps, Velcro®, foam tubing, or easy to grasp knobs; and/or using color or shape cues.

3. *Changing task expectations.* Strategies for changing task expectations include requiring a less sophisticated response (e.g., using two hands rather than one, completing only the first step of the task, using a single word rather than a sentence) or accepting a response in a different modality (e.g., pointing rather than verbalizing, holding up a picture rather than giving a verbal response).

4. *Arranging peer assistance.* The classroom staff can arrange opportunities for peers to demonstrate desired behaviors (e.g., sharing, taking turns) and help one another. One of the primary advantages of inclusive settings is the availability of typically developing peers. Staff should structure activities so that these peers have opportunities and know how to invite children with special needs to join their activities in meaningful ways. Teachers can facilitate the children learning from peers by pointing out and describing specific behaviors for the children with disabilities to imitate (e.g., "Look how Jason is taking the scissors from the can on the table").

Figure 2: Adaptations, Supports, and Data Collection for Adam

Child: _Adam_   Date: _8-23-02_

Adaptations, Supports, and Data Collection Form

Objectives (List Briefly)	Description of Adaptations and Supports — Describe *how* you will: (1) provide scaffolding and practice; (2) adapt the task/modify materials, (3) change the task expectations, and/or (4) arrange peer assistance.	Person Responsible	Data Collection Opportunities and Procedures
Greet teacher	Step in front of the door and make eye contact; provide a model for "Hi" and for a response to "How are you?" If no response, move aside to let him enter.	Selina	2 opps per day (morning & recess) Record/tally on matrix
Choose toy or activity	Display 2 toys (preferred and nonpreferred). Prompt choice making; provide toy and guide Adam to the table. Do same with photos of activities.	Selina	4 opps per day Record on matrix
Play cooperatively with peers	Sit with Adam and a peer; introduce activities that require two players. Prompt Adam to take a turn and then wait for peer to act. Praise cooperative efforts.	Lisa	4 opps per day Note on cards or sticky notes
Respond verbally to roll call	Change response requirement to one word ("Here"); provide a model.	Selina	1 opp per day Record on matrix
Respond to questions about a story	Adapt the task: provide a picture board with copies of the story pictures. Ask comprehension questions that can be answered by pointing to a picture.	Lisa	1 opp per day Note on cards or sticky notes
Retrieve art materials	Peer assistance: Ask a peer to remind Adam by saying, "Follow me to get our supplies." Prompt if necessary by saying, "Go with ____ to get your supplies from the table."	Lisa	1 opp per day Note on cards or sticky notes

Step 6: Decide Who Will Provide the Adaptations and Supports

Even if there are only two adults in the classroom, it is important to be clear about who has responsibility for assisting with and teaching the skill in each of the activities. Then the responsible adult can be focused on the child and be prepared to provide the needed adaptation and/or support when an opportunity arises for practice of the target behavior. Note that in Figure 2 either Lisa or Selina, the two adults who are present on a daily basis in Adam's class, is listed in the third column as the responsible adult.

Step 7: Plan Data Collection Opportunities and Procedures

Regardless of whether there is only one opportunity in a typical school day for a target behavior to be performed (e.g., responding to roll call) or numerous practice opportunities (e.g., sharing and taking turns), data collection is a challenge (McLean & Hanline, 1990; Odom & McEvoy, 1988). A simple strategy is to jot notes on sticky labels or pads, index cards, or in a small spiral-bound notebook. These can be carried (with a pencil) in a pocket or mounted in relevant activity areas.

A matrix provides space for recording data. Figure 3 shows the matrix developed for Adam. His objectives are listed across the horizontal axis and daily activities are listed on the vertical axis. There is a second page for the remaining activities in Adam's school day, which is not shown. Each cell provides space to record opportunities and responses (whether independent or prompted) and/or write a comment about the behavior. Adam's teacher printed the matrix on transparency film. She records data with a marker that can be erased each afternoon after the day's observations have been transferred to a permanent record in Adam's portfolio. There is a folder in Adam's portfolio for each of his objectives.

Some days there may be events such as a holiday celebration, a field trip, or a substitute teacher that interfere with data collection. This should not be considered a problem. It is sufficient to collect data on a subset of the objectives each day. Adam's teachers aim for at least three days of data for each objective each week. Once placed in the portfolio, these data provide a visible record of Adam's learning experiences and his progress toward objectives. They also support the teachers' efforts to plan and provide developmentally appropriate activities and routines.

Conclusion

Neisworth and Bagnato (1996) outline four preferred practices in assessment (from the National Association for the Education of Young

Figure 3: Data Collection Matrix for Adam

	Greet Teacher	Choose Toy/Activity	Cooperation With Peers	Respond to Roll	Respond to Questions	Get Art Materials
Arrival						
Circle						
Art						
Snack						

Children [NAEYC] and the National Association of Early Childhood Specialists in State Departments of Education [NAECSSDE]). Assessment should: (1) demonstrate child learning in relation to the curriculum goals and objectives; (2) guide individualized instruction based on children's abilities and interests; (3) help teachers match learning activities to children's abilities and interests; and (4) include a systematic means for collecting data that is useful for planning and meaningful to parents. One of the challenges of achieving the goals of early childhood inclusion is assessment that generates meaningful goals and objectives. The Ecological Assessment and Planning Process meets all of those criteria. This process generates goals and objectives for young children in inclusive preschools that reflect meaningful and functional skills, facilitate participation and independence in developmentally appropriate settings, and derive from and thus can be taught in the context of classroom routines and activities.

Note
You can reach Linda McCormick by e-mail at mccormic@hawaii.edu

References
Barker, R. G. (1968). *Ecological psychology*. Stanford, CA: Stanford University Press.
Bredekamp, S., & Copple, C. (1997). *Developmentally appropriate practice in early childhood programs* (Rev. ed.). Washington, DC: National Association for the Education of Young Children (NAEYC).
Bronfenbrenner, U. (1977). Toward an experimental ecology of human behavior. *American Psychologist, 32*, 513–531.
Bronfenbrenner, U. (1979). *The ecology of human development: Experiments by nature and design*. Cambridge: Harvard University Press.
Brown, L., Branston, M. B., Hamre-Nietupski, S., Pumpian, I., Certo, N., & Gruenewald, L. (1979). A strategy for developing chronological age-appropriate and functional curricular content for severely handicapped adolescents and young adults. *Journal of Special Education, 13*, 81–90.
Edmiaston, R., Dolezal, V., Doolittle, S., Erickson, C., & Merritt, S. (2000). Developing individualized educational programs for children in inclusive settings: A developmentally appropriate framework. *Young Children, 55*(4), 36–41.
Grisham-Brown, J., & Hemmeter, M. L. (1998). Writing IEP goals and objectives: Reflecting an activity-based approach to instruction for young children with disabilities. *Young Exceptional Children, 3*(1), 2–10.
Haney, M., & Cavallaro, C. C. (1996). Using ecological assessment in daily program planning for children with disabilities in typical preschool settings. *Topics in Early Childhood Special Education, 16*, 76–81.
McCormick, L., & Noonan, M. J. (1996). A "can do" inventory for three-year olds. *Teaching Exceptional Children, 28*(2), 14–17.
McCormick, L., Wong, M., & Yogi, L. (2002). *Individualization in the inclusive classroom: A planning process*. Manuscript submitted for publication.
McLean, M., & Hanline, M. F. (1990). Providing early intervention services in integrated environments: Challenges and opportunities for the future. *Topics in Early Childhood Special Education, 10*, 62-77.
Neisworth, J. T., & Bagnato, S. (1996). Assessment for early intervention: Emerging themes and practices. In S. L. Odom & M. E. McLean (Eds.), *Early intervention/early childhood special education recommended practices* (pp. 223–257). Austin, TX: Pro-Ed.
Odom, S. L., & McEvoy, M. A. (1988). Integration of young children with handicaps and normally developing children. In S. Odom & M. Karnes (Eds.), *Early intervention for infants and children with handicaps: An empirical base* (pp. 241–268). Baltimore: Paul H. Brookes.
Vygotsky, L. (1978). *Mind in society: The development of higher psychological processes*. Cambridge: Harvard University Press.

Dynamic Assessment

Understanding Children's Development

Vera Joanna Burton, M.A.,
University of Illinois at Urbana-Champaign

Ruth V. Watkins, Ph.D.,
University of Illinois at Urbana-Champaign

Call for Increased Assessment

In recent years, assessment has become a key focus of discussion and initiatives throughout education. One of the main goals of the educational initiative, "No Child Left Behind" (2002) is to ensure that students are reaching identified educational objectives. This goal necessitates increased evaluation of student progress. Teachers, administrators, and school personnel are now attempting to meet standards and expectations for assessment that provides meaningful information on student progress.

In one inner city kindergarten classroom, a new teacher is preparing for the upcoming school year. Ms. Johnson is excited to put her educational coursework into practice. Will her students be able to reach her high expectations? Will she live up to theirs? Ms. Johnson reviews her students' vocabulary test scores gathered during kindergarten screening in order to begin preparing her reading curriculum. After all, research has shown that early vocabulary tests are a good predictor of later reading skills (Snow, Burns, & Griffin, 1998). She becomes concerned as she notices student after student performing below average expectations on the vocabulary tests. In fact, the class average is about ten points below average. Looking into the preschool records for those students who had attended Head Start (about half the class), Ms. Johnson notices one or two students identified with language disabilities; however, many of the students with low vocabulary test scores had been reaching classroom expectations the previous year. There was no evidence of teacher or parent concerns about vocabulary. Ms. Johnson knows that static standardized vocabulary measures often provide incomplete information for students from low income backgrounds. And what of the children who did not attend Head Start and were just starting school? She wonders how she can get a more complete picture of her incoming students, particularly their strengths and needs in the area of language development.

Static Testing Versus Dynamic Testing

Conventional forms of assessment, primarily static testing, focus on independent performance. Dynamic assessment, on the other hand, focuses on process rather than performance. It is more readily incorporated into teaching and intervention and may also assist in the identification of developmentally appropriate goals.

Traditional static measures such as the *Kaufman Assessment Battery for Children* (*K-ABC*) (Kaufman & Kaufman, 1983) identify current levels of functioning. In other words, they identify knowledge or skills a child has already mastered. Teachers often use information about skills that a child has mastered along with the target curriculum or the child's IEP/IFSP to guide their decisions about the next areas to cover during intervention. However, static assessment may not be optimal for identifying which abilities the child is most ready to learn next. Furthermore, static assessment is difficult to incorporate within the learning environment. Of additional concern is that recent literature has identified many static measures, particularly those measuring language skills, as inappropriate for students from culturally and linguistically diverse backgrounds (Stockman, 2000; Washington & Craig, 1992, 1999). This inappropriateness stems from the fact that many of the static measures currently in use do not assess mastery of skills independent of experience-based knowledge. For example, speech-language pathologists use standardized static vocabulary tests to measure both word knowledge and word-learning ability by measuring words the child already knows. These kinds of tests tap previous experience with the words in the test in addition to word-learning ability. Although static tests provide teachers and parents with a look at current ability, these measures don't provide information about how well the child will learn new words. Children from nonmainstream families may have had varying amounts of experience with the test words, and, therefore, such static measures are vulnerable to error in terms of diagnosing language difference as language disability.

A similar situation exists with the assessment of children's abilities in virtually every other developmental domain. Static measures of

> *Conventional forms of assessment, primarily static testing, focus on independent performance.*

young children's abilities in cognitive, social, adaptive, and motor domains tend to predominate in the field (McLean, Bailey, & Wolery, 1996). Despite the many strengths of these measurement tools, they are generally of limited assistance in: (1) guiding decisions about skills the child is ready to learn, and (2) providing direction for classroom-based interventions.

Dynamic assessment, on the other hand, helps to identify any skills a child is in the process of mastering or is able to perform with the help of an adult or peer. By identifying skills that are in reach for the child, time may be more effectively used to target skill areas in which the child is ready to move ahead. Additionally, in many cases, the design of dynamic assessment allows it to take place during instruction and in the context of natural everyday events. Finally, dynamic assessment has particular promise for describing the skills of children from low income and other nonmainstream backgrounds including those from families speaking languages other than English because the assessment method is not experience dependent (Peña, Iglesias, & Lidz, 2001; Ukrainetz, Harpell, Walsh, & Coyle, 2000). Dynamic assessment measures the learning process rather than the current performance. Therefore, it provides teachers and parents with information about a child's ability to learn a new skill rather than about past experiences.

Dynamic assessment, on the other hand, helps to identify any skills a child is in the process of mastering or is able to perform with the help of an adult or peer. By identifying skills that are in reach for the child, time may be more effectively used to target skill areas in which the child is ready to move ahead.

Dynamic Assessment

Dynamic assessment has been recommended for use in the fields of education, psychology, and speech-language pathology. The assessment measures a concept referred to as the *zone of proximal development*, described by Vygotsky in the 1930s. Vygotsky (1978) believed that because learning and development were interrelated, a complete picture of a child's developmental level could only be obtained by characterizing the child's actual development retrospectively (using static measures) and potential development prospectively (using dynamic measures). The difference between these two developmental levels is termed the zone of proximal development. In other words, it is the difference between what a child can achieve independently and what can be achieved with help.

Measuring the zone of proximal development through dynamic assessment could be used for multiple purposes. First, dynamic assessment could be used to develop teaching or intervention techniques. Second, such a measure could be used as an assessment of a child's dynamic developmental state, predicting the immediate future development of the child (Vygotsky, 1978). For use as a teaching technique, Vygotsky believed that children learn through interactive stages with the adult doing most of the work in the first stage, the adult and the child sharing the responsibility in the second stage, and the child working unaided in the final stage. The final stage of learning is termed the *actual developmental level* and is measured by traditional static assessments. A teacher's role at each of these stages is different and the teacher must be able to make ongoing decisions about what level of help is appropriate during intervention (Schneider & Watkins, 1996). For use as an evaluation tool, Vygotsky intended dynamic assessment to be used to supplement static assessment with information about developing skills and readiness, in balance with information about actual developmental levels.

Measuring the zone of proximal development through dynamic assessment could be used for multiple purposes.

There are two common forms of dynamic assessment: (1) test-teach-retest, and (2) successive cueing (Campione, Brown, Ferrara, & Bryant, 1984). Test-teach-retest has been used to measure important language areas such as story-telling ability and vocabulary skills. Successive cueing has been used to measure language skills such as word-learning ability, and to predict use of two-word combinations. In addition, both approaches to dynamic assessment can be applied to measuring young children's development across a range of domains. Examples of both test-teach-retest and successive cueing are provided following.

Test-Teach-Retest

Test-teach-retest is a method similar to diagnostic teaching and allows a teacher to identify if either an intervention or an evaluating tool is appropriate for students (see Campione et al., 1984). A child is first given a pretest to establish the current unaided level of functioning. The pretest is followed by mediated learning experiences, in which the evaluator provides skill training or strategy training (Feuerstein, 1980). Skill training is defined as instructing the child on prerequisite skills necessary to complete the task (e.g., working on sight word vocabulary or basic addition facts needed to solve a story problem). Strategy training is making the child aware of what the test requires (e.g., teaching the child to draw a picture to help solve the story problem). After mediation, the child is retested. The difference between the pre- and post-test is thought to define the zone of proximal development.

By determining what skills are within a child's zone of proximal development, the test-teach-retest method can be used to identify if a child is developmentally responsive to a particular intervention technique. If the task is within the child's zone of proximal development, the mediated learning experiences should improve performance on the task. If the child's performance does not improve, the intervention used during the mediated learning session was not appropriate or the task was not developmentally appropriate for the child. This information can be used to identify appropriate intervention strategies for the child and to help determine target skills for intervention.

For example, in the area of preacademic mathematics, a preschool teacher is attempting to teach one-to-one correspondence to Peter. She takes the opportunity to work with him during the week that he is the snack helper. On Monday (test), the teacher says, "Peter, I need you to put a plate, napkin, and cup by each student's place." Peter manages to get the supplies to the table, but places them in a big pile near one end of the table. The next day at snack time (teach), the teacher assists Peter using both skill training and strategy training. First, she and Peter place a plate in front of each chair, saying, "A plate for Mike, a plate for Ashley … " until  there is plate for each student. Then they repeat this procedure for the napkins and the cups. Practicing the skills needed for one-to-one correspondence while using the strategy of a verbal routine and the plates as a guide, Peter is successful at setting the table. On Wednesday (retest), the teacher asks Peter to place the plates on the table and to put one napkin on top of each plate, which he does. Then she asks him to distribute the cups in the same way. Instead, Peter again places the cups near one end of the table. Using this informal test-teach-retest, the teacher is able to identify that the skill of one-to-one correspondence is sensitive to instruction for Peter. He has not yet mastered the skill and it is, therefore, appropriate for intervention.

In the area of language skills, Peña and colleagues (Peña et al., 2001; Peña, Quinn, & Iglesias, 1992) used the test-teach-retest method to measure the amount of change in picture labeling brought about by two 20-minute small group sessions. These researchers believed that the preschool children in the study were not required to label extensively at home and that picture labeling was not an appropriate task without mediation. Following the two mediated learning sessions, the children were retested on the picture labeling subtest. Those who were identified as typically developing made significant improvements. Those who were identified as having language delays continued to have difficulty with the task and made very little progress between the test and retest.

Successive Cueing

There is no pre- and post-test format in the successive cueing model. Instead, scaffolding or gradual prompting is provided to assist the child in task completion (see Campione et al., 1984). The child is given a task to complete. At first, no help is provided. If the child is unable to complete the task, progressively more direct help is provided until the child is able to perform the task or until a direct model has been provided and the child has not had success. The amount of help necessary is the measure of the zone of proximal development. If a child makes significant gains with limited assistance, he or she is not considered to have difficulty with the

There is no pre- and post-test format in the successive cueing model.

task or is considered ready to work on the skill in question. The information provided by a dynamic assessment together with a static assessment can aid in determining the necessity or course of intervention.

In a preschool classroom, teachers often aim to promote successful social interactions between peers when use of materials and toys is negotiated, rather than requiring adult mediation. Successive cueing could be used to evaluate young children's readiness to socially negotiate with peers, as well as promote peer exchanges. For example, Jamie, Jenna, and Jamal each want a turn to use a desired toy, a toy that is in use by another child. Each expresses this desire by approaching their teacher with a request. The teacher begins with a high-level redirecting cue, such as, "Go ask Mike for a turn." Only Jamal successfully approaches Mike and gains a turn; both Jamie and Jenna move to another play area. Later, Jamie and Jenna again approach their teacher with a request to use the toy. This time, the teacher provides a more direct cue, such as, "Say, 'Mike, it's my turn now.'" Following this level of assistance, Jenna approaches Mike directly, asks for a turn, and succeeds. Jamie watches from a distance, but does not approach the other children to ask for a turn. Later, Jamie again asks the teacher for a chance to use the toy. This time, the teacher and Jamie together approach the child using the toy. The teacher prompts, "Jamie, tell Mike, 'It's my turn now.'" With this direct level of assistance, Jamie succeeds in socially interacting with his classmate and in gaining access to the desired activity.

In a research investigation of the successive cueing approach, Bain and Olswang (1995) developed a cueing model for predicting potential for immediate language change when children were progressing from one-word to two-word speech. In general, Olswang and Bain (1996) found that the dynamic assessment procedure predicted better than static measures which children would show significant language gains. That is, the young children who were most responsive to the least directive adult cues were likely to progress more swiftly to two-word combinations in their spontaneous speech. The likelihood of swift increase in children's language skills was more closely linked to responsiveness to cueing than to scores on standardized language tests.

Although the methods of test-teach-retest and successive cueing differ, the same principle directs both approaches. They are an attempt to measure potential for change or modifiability. Neither approach measures static knowledge, which can be experience-dependent. An additional aspect of dynamic assessment is that it is focused on the conditions under which performance can be changed instead of on only the performance itself. The assessment focuses on the interaction of the assessor and the examinee, the influence of this interaction on performance, and the responsiveness of the examinee to the interaction (Lidz, 1991).

An additional aspect of dynamic assessment is that it is focused on the conditions under which performance can be changed instead of on only the performance itself.

Dynamic Assessment as a Diagnostic Tool

Dynamic assessment methods are being developed for diagnostic use as well. There is increasing evidence that both successive cueing measures and test-teach-retest measures can accurately predict modifiability for children from the various language backgrounds that exist in the United States. In several empirical studies, both methods have also shown some promise regarding their ability to differentiate between typically developing children and those with disabilities (Bain & Olswang, 1995;

Gutierrez-Clellen, Conroy, Brown, & Robinson-Zanartu, 1998; Peña et al., 1992, 2001). Although these methods are only in the early stages of development, teachers may find using informal dynamic assessment to be informative. In many cases, simple modifications or new record-keeping techniques can embed dynamic assessment measures into currently used static and authentic assessment tools or curriculum and interventions.

Developing Your Own Dynamic Assessment

Test-Teach-Retest

A teacher or parent can readily modify existing static tests or other tasks to fit the test-teach-retest model of dynamic assessment. First, a task is given to the child, without assistance, as a pre-test. If the child is unable to perform the task independently, the teacher or parent completes a task analysis, dissecting the skill into small teachable steps (see Moyer & Dardig, 1978 for a complete description of a task analysis). The teacher or parent then spends one or two brief mediation sessions working with the child on skill and/or strategy training. Skill training is provided to assist the child in developing any prerequisite skills necessary for task

completion. In addition, the teacher or parent might work on strategy training in order to make the child more aware of any strategies that can assist in task performance. The final step is to repeat the initial task assessment in the form of a post-test.

An informal example of the test-teach-retest approach could occur when a parent and preschooler are working together on a puzzle. The parent observes that, working alone, the child is not able to successfully place any pieces in the puzzle. The child appears interested in the activity, but seems to approach the task very randomly and is quickly frustrated. In a mediated fashion, while the parent and child work together, the parent provides strategy training by identifying several helpful strategies for puzzle completion, such as suggesting that the child begin by placing the edge pieces (i.e., the ones that have "straight" sides), then finding colors that "match" and putting them together, and finally, looking for "bumps" and "grooves" in puzzle pieces that could go together. The parent and child practice these strategies with several different puzzles, providing the opportunity for skill acquisition. In a subsequent play session, the parent begins by observing the child's approach to the puzzle. The parent notes that the child is now considerably more successful in completing the puzzle alone and is beginning to use the strategies that the parent modeled.

Successive Cueing

After selecting a desired task, the teacher or parent identifies a series of helping cues along a hierarchy of least to most assistance. The task is then presented to the child. If the child is unable to complete the task independently, the teacher or parent begins providing the least amount of help and continues to provide additional levels of help until either the child is able to complete the task or the teacher or parent has provided a direct model. If the child is able to complete the task independently, the child's actual developmental level has been measured. If the child cannot complete the task even with the highest level of help, then this task is not yet appropriate for the child to learn. If the child is able to perform the task with some amount of help, this is a good indication that the task is within the child's zone of proximal development and is appropriate for teaching. The amount of help required for the child to succeed provides information about his or her readiness to learn the skill.

The amount of help required for the child to succeed provides information about his or her readiness to learn the skill.

Recall the earlier example in which the teacher aimed to promote children's social interactions. The teacher informally offered three levels of assistance, one that provided limited aid (i.e., "Go ask Mike for a turn"), one that provided a moderate amount of guidance (i.e., "Say, 'Mike, it's my turn now'"), and one that provided an immediate and direct model (i.e., accompanying the child and modeling, "Tell Mike, 'It's my turn now'"). The amount of assistance the child needs in order to be successful in socially negotiating with peers is the informative feature.

Follow-Up in the Kindergarten Classroom

After investigating a number of assessment options, the concerned kindergarten teacher, Ms. Johnson, decides to create a dynamic assessment that will provide her with additional information about the word-learning skills of her students. She believes that the test-teach-retest method is most appropriate for two purposes: determining (1) if a static assessment tool is assessing what it is supposed to assess, and (2) if an intervention is working. Ms. Johnson thinks that the successive cueing method, on the other hand, is most appropriate for

Table 1: Successive Cueing Strategy

Cue Number	Score	Cue	Example
Cue One	4.0	Elicitation Question	Noun: "What is that?"
Cue Two	3.0	Elicitation With Reference	Noun: "Remember in the story, this was the thing that …. What is it called?"
Cue Three	2.0	Elicitation in Cloze Format	Noun: "It starts with a 'c.'"
Cue Four	1.0	Elicitation With Model	Noun: "This is a ____. What is it?"
No Response/ Incorrect Response	0.0		

identifying a child's potential for learning a new task. The teacher decides to use the following successive cueing strategy to tap the word-learning ability of her kindergartners. Successive cueing has previously revealed intact word-learning abilities in children from low income backgrounds even when scores on static vocabulary measures were below average expectations (Burton, 2002).

While the teaching assistant, Mr. Smith, supervises centers for the rest of the class, Ms. Johnson meets individually with each student. The task begins with the teacher reading a picture book to the child. Eight examples of four made-up words appear in the story. Following the story, the child is provided with toys that correspond to the objects depicted by the made-up words in the story. The child is encouraged to play with the toys while Ms. Johnson asks the child to name the objects, using the made-up words. She follows the least to most direct cues shown in Table 1.

First Ms. Johnson attempts to have the child name the made-up word by pointing to an object and asking the participant to name the object with no help by saying, "Can you tell me what this is?" If the child responds correctly, Ms. Johnson replies, "Yes, that is a ____." If the child does not respond or responds incorrectly, Ms. Johnson provides the prompt of context by finding a picture of the item in the book and helping the child to recall something about the item by stating, "Remember, this was the thing that ___" and again asks for the child to name the object. If the child still cannot recall the made-up word, Ms. Johnson provides a phonemic cue by stating, "It begins with ___" and again asks for the participant to name the object. The final cue Ms. Johnson provides is a direct model in which she states, "It is a ___" and then asks the child to name the object.

The majority of the students in the kindergarten class are able to label the objects with their made-up names when provided with the help. The successive cueing strategy enables Ms. Johnson to determine that word learning through storybook reading and without direct instruction is within most of the children's zones of proximal development. The dynamic assessment also allows the teacher to examine potential word-learning ability without tapping previous knowledge of real words. Finally, the use of the dynamic assessment measure in conjunction with the traditional static measure provides a much more complete picture of the students' development—both past learning and current potential—and greatly informs Ms. Johnson's reading curriculum.

Conclusion

In summary, this article has presented the promise that dynamic assessment offers teachers and parents to better understand young children's developmental strengths and needs in a range of domains. Despite these strengths, it is important to note that formal applications of dynamic assessment are not yet widely used in the field of early childhood education and that additional research is needed to fully realize the potential of this tool. Existing assessment tools are diverse in the manner in which they apply the dynamic principles, and more information, such as normative data that can guide approaches to utilizing dynamic methods, are needed (see Lidz & Elliot, 2000; Miller, Gilliam, & Peña, 2001 for examples of current dynamic assessment models). That is, the development of published tools that provide information about the amount of change or modifiability expected for various groups of young children would be very useful for the field (see Miller, Gilliam, & Peña,

... This article has presented the promise that dynamic assessment offers teachers and parents to better understand young children's developmental strengths and needs in a range of domains.

2001 for an example of such a procedure). Clearly additional research will be informative and will yield innovative applications of dynamic approaches to assessing children's skills; however, there is ample evidence that the dynamic methods of test-teach-retest and successive cueing can effectively and informatively be applied to current challenges in early childhood assessment. In the classroom and at home, dynamic approaches yield essential insights about children's abilities and future development.

Notes

You can reach Vera Joanna Burton by e-mail at vjburton@uiuc.edu

Partial support for the preparation of this manuscript was provided by USDE/OSED Grant #H325001009 (R. Watkins, PI) and the Robert L. Sprague Thesis Award.

References

Bain, B., & Olswang, L. (1995). Examining readiness for learning two-word utterances by children with specific expressive language impairment: Dynamic assessment validation. *American Journal of Speech-Language Pathology, 4*, 81–91.

Burton, V. J. (2002). *Dynamic QUIL assessment as a measure of word-learning ability.* Unpublished master's thesis, University of Illinois, Urbana-Champaign.

Campione, J. C., Brown, A. L., Ferrara, R. A., & Bryant, N. R. (1984). The zone of proximal development: Implications for individual differences and learning. In B. Rogoff & J. V. Wertsch (Eds.), *Children's learning in the "zone of proximal development"* (pp. 77–91). Washington, DC: Jossey-Bass.

Feuerstein, R. (1980). *Instructional enrichment: An intervention program for cognitive modifiability.* Baltimore: University Park Press.

Gutierrez-Clellen, V. F., Conroy, B., Brown, S., & Robinson-Zanartu, C. (1998). Modifiability: A dynamic approach to assessing immediate language change. *Journal of Children's Communication Development, 19*(2), 31–42.

Kaufman, A. S., & Kaufman, N. L. (1983). *Kaufman Assessment Battery for Children.* Circle Pines, MN: American Guidance Service.

Lidz, C. S. (1991). *Practitioner's guide to dynamic assessment.* New York: Guilford.

Lidz,, C. S., & Elliot, J. G. (Eds.). (2000). *Dynamic assessment: Prevailing models and applications.* New York: JAI.

McLean, M., Bailey, D. B., & Wolery, M. (Eds.). (1996). *Assessing infants and preschoolers with special needs* (2nd ed.). Columbus, OH: Merrill/Prentice Hall.

Miller, L., Gillam, R., & Peña, E. (2001). *Using dynamic assessment and intervention to improve children's narrative skills.* Austin, TX: Pro-Ed.

Moyer, J. R., & Dardig, J. C. (1978). Practical task analysis for special educators. *Teaching Exceptional Children, 11*(1), 16–18.

No Child Left Behind Act of 2001, P.L. 107–110, 115 Stat. 1425 (2002).

Olswang, L. B., & Bain, B. A. (1996). Assessment information for predicting upcoming change in language production. *Journal of Speech and Hearing Research, 39*, 414-423.

Peña, E., Iglesias, A., & Lidz, C. (2001). Reducing test bias through dynamic assessment of children's word-learning ability. *American Journal of Speech-Language Pathology, 10*, 138–154.

Peña, E., Quinn, R., & Iglesias, A. (1992). The application of dynamic methods to language assessment: A nonbiased procedure. *Journal of Special Education, 26*, 269–280.

Schneider, P., & Watkins, R. V. (1996). Applying Vygotskian developmental theory to language intervention. *Language, Speech, and Hearing Services in Schools, 27*, 157–170.

Snow, C. E., Burns, M. S., & Griffin, P. (Eds.). (1998). *Preventing reading difficulties in young children.* Washington, DC: National Academy Press.

Stockman, I. (2000). The new Peabody Picture Vocabulary Test-III: An illusion of unbiased assessment? *Language, Speech, and Hearing Services in Schools, 31*, 340–353.

Ukrainetz, T. A., Harpell, S., Walsh, C., & Coyle, C. (2000). A preliminary investigation of dynamic assessment with Native American kindergartners. *Language, Speech, and Hearing Services in the Schools, 31*, 142–154.

Vygotsky, L. S. (1978). *Mind in society: The development of higher psychological processes.* Cambridge: Harvard University Press.

Washington, J., & Craig, H. (1992). Performances of low income African American preschool and kindergarten children on the Peabody Picture Vocabulary Test-Revised. *Language, Speech, and Hearing Services in Schools, 23*, 329–333.

Washington, J., & Craig, H. (1999). Performances of at-risk African American preschoolers on the Peabody Picture Vocabulary Test-III. *Language, Speech, and Hearing Services in Schools, 30*, 75–82.

Assessing Young Children for Whom English Is a Second Language

Mary McLean, Ph.D., University of Wisconsin, Milwaukee

T he population of children and families in the United States who receive early childhood education or early childhood special education services is becoming increasingly diverse (Children's Defense Fund, 1989). In a survey of Head Start programs conducted by the Administration for Children, Youth, and Families in 1994, 91% of the responding programs reported an increase in at least one cultural or linguistic group in the previous five years (Tabors, 1998). The evaluation and assessment of young children who are culturally and linguistically diverse presents significant challenges to early childhood professionals. When the outcome of assessment is determination of eligibility for special education services, the cost of error is greatly increased. The fact that the number of children in special education who are culturally and linguistically diverse is higher than expected may be reflective of the potential for error in the assessment process (Yansen & Shulman, 1996). It is also possible, however, for children who need early intervention services to go unserved because of the difficulty of distinguishing between cultural and linguistic differences and the presence of a disability. Screening and assessment practices must be carefully evaluated in terms of cultural or language biases that could cause either over- or underrepresentation of children from various cultural and linguistic groups.

Linguistic Diversity

All young children in the age range of birth through age eight are still in the process of acquiring their first language. The effect of acquiring a second language on a child's language, cognitive, and social development can be quite complex. Professionals who engage in the assessment of young children who are learning English as a second language frequently experience frustration in the selection of appropriate assessment instruments and strategies. There are suggested guidelines, however, which can help the assessment team plan and implement assessment procedures in a way that will yield diagnostically helpful information.

Children who are bilingual are a heterogeneous group; the degree of proficiency achieved in both languages will vary depending on when and how extensively the child has been exposed to the languages. Bilingualism is often described according to the age of acquisition of the second language, environmental influences on the language, and the degree of proficiency in the languages. "Simultaneous bilingualism" refers to the child who has heard two languages since birth; "preschool successive bilingualism" refers to the child who learns a second language after age three; "school-age successive bilingualism" refers to the child who learns another language after the age of five (Moore & Beatty, 1995).

Kayser (1989) reminds us that the degree of bilingual proficiency actually achieved by a child will depend on many factors, including linguistic, social, emotional, political, demographic, and cultural factors. It has also been suggested that the match between teaching style and learning style may be a factor once children are in educational programs (Barrera, 1993; Kayser, 1993). While in the past it was believed that learning a second language may be detrimental to the development of the child's first language, it is now generally believed that bilingualism may actually enhance cognitive and social development (Hakuta, 1986; McCardle, Kim, Grube, & Randall, 1995). However, the possibility that learning a second language may actually result in a temporary lack of proficiency in both languages is very real

The effect of acquiring a second language on a child's language, cognitive, and social development can be quite complex.

and must be seriously considered as assessment teams are evaluating a child for a possible language delay or disorder (Schiff-Meyers, 1992).

Limited English proficiency alone is not sufficient reason for referring a child for assessment for special education services. Similarly, as indicated previously, a lack of proficiency or delay in the native language also is not sufficient reason for making a referral. In considering whether or not to refer a young child who is learning English as a second language for assessment for special education, early childhood educators should consider whether the child is having difficulty communicating effectively at home or in the cultural community. Observations of the child's progress or lack of progress in learning English in comparison to peers who are also learning English should also be considered (Billings,

Pearson, Gill, & Shureen, 1997). However, once the decision is made to refer a child for assessment, much information needs to be gathered so the assessment team can make an informed decision.

Assessment procedures for children who are linguistically diverse must by necessity be different from typical assessment procedures (Lund & Duchan, 1993; Mattes & Omark, 1991; Roseberry-McKibben, 1994). Many of the recommended practices for children who are English mono-lingual are also recommended for children who are learning English as a second language. For example, using multiple measures, gathering information in a natural environment, using a multidisciplinary team approach, and using a family-centered approach are all recommended (Bondurant-Utz, 1994). However, the necessity of achieving assessment results that are not biased by the child's language or cultural diversity will require careful selection of instruments and strategies. The linguistic background of the child must be understood so the team can consider the possibility of language loss or arrested language development due to the development of the second language (Schiff-Meyers, 1992).

According to Yansen and Shulman (1996), the team must follow a sequential process of assessment with children who are linguistically diverse which begins with assessing the child's language dominance and proficiency of skills in all languages. Language proficiency refers to the child's fluency and competence in using a particular language. Language dominance refers to the language the child prefers to speak and that the child speaks most proficiently at the time of assessment (Roseberry-McKibben, 1994). Since the Individuals with Disabilities Education Act (IDEA) requires testing to be done in the language or mode of communication in which the child is most proficient, most school systems administer a language dominance measure to determine which language should be used for assessment. Unfortunately, determining language dominance can be quite complex and frequently cannot be reduced to a simple test of language skill in two languages (Kayser, 1989). Language dominance may vary depending on the aspect of language that is being assessed.

Limited English proficiency alone is not sufficient reason for referring a child for assessment for special education services.

In addition, the context in which the assessment is completed may affect the young child's use of language. Roseberry-McKibben (1994) suggests measuring proficiency should consist of: (1) completion of a language background questionnaire by the parents or caregivers, (2) teacher and parent or caregiver interviews, and (3) scores on both direct language assessment and observation measures. Kayser (1989) recommends the use of a systematic and quantifiable observation procedure with support from questionnaires administered to the parents and caregivers.

However, assessing the child only in the language which appears to be the dominant language may not be the best practice. Barrera Metz (1991) stresses that children should be assessed in both L1 (the native language or primary language) and L2 (the acquired language). She warns that the practice of testing only in the dominant language does not yield all the information needed since it will not allow the assessment team to consider the effect that acquiring L2 may be having on L1.

Furthermore, rather than assessing only vocabulary and grammar in both languages, it is recommended that proficiency tests focus on communication competence which includes, according to Ortiz (1984), the ability to use the language functionally in conversation with peers and adults both in school and at home.

For children who are learning to read and write, additional information may be needed. Roseberry-McKibben (1994) warns that the practice of assessing proficiency only in speaking and listening, as opposed to reading and writing, may lead to misinterpretation of a child's needs. Basic conversational skills develop more quickly in second language acquisition than written language proficiency which can take five to seven years to achieve a level commensurate with native speakers. Children who are found to be proficient in English on the basis of a test of conversational skills in English may have great difficulty with written English and therefore may incorrectly be found to need special education. Unless the assessment team is aware of the impact of second language learning on a child's skill with written English, the child may be incorrectly diagnosed as having a disability and therefore eligible for special education.

Language proficiency refers to the child's fluency and competence in using a particular language. Language dominance refers to the language the child prefers to speak and that the child speaks most proficiently at the time of assessment ....

Gathering Prereferral Information

According to Ortiz and Maldonado-Colon (1986), the key to reducing inappropriate special education placements is to reduce inappropriate referrals for evaluation. Early childhood educators need to carefully

Table 1: Checklist of Information Needed Prior to Referral for Evaluation for Special Education

	Yes	No
1. Adequate information about the language dominance and proficiency of family members has been obtained and, if needed, an interpreter/translator has been identified to facilitate communication with the family.	☐	☐
2. Information about the language dominance and proficiency of other caregivers or children who interact routinely with the child has been identified.	☐	☐
3. The family has been asked to share their impressions of the child's development.	☐	☐
4. With the family's permission, other service providers and caregivers have been asked to share their impressions of the child's development.	☐	☐
5. If needed, a cultural guide has been asked to help interpret the child's behavior.	☐	☐
6. All developmental domains, including hearing and vision, have been screened.	☐	☐
7. Screening for language proficiency and dominance has been completed.	☐	☐
8. The child has been observed both in the early childhood setting and at home.	☐	☐
9. The child has had sufficient time to become accustomed to the linguistic and social environment of the early childhood setting.	☐	☐
10. The child's social, cognitive, and motor skills have been observed in situations where language comprehension is not required.	☐	☐

collect and analyze information on a young child who is culturally and linguistically diverse prior to making the initial referral for assessment of eligibility for special education. Information about the child's development, the sociocultural context of the child's family, and a comparison of the child's development to the developmental patterns of other children from a similar background can be helpful. Based on the work of Billings et al. (1997) and Langdon (1989), the checklist presented in Table 1 can assist the early childhood educator in ensuring that a referral is based on complete information about the child.

Selection of Instruments/Strategies

The Division for Early Childhood recommended practices for assessment (Neisworth & Bagnato, 1996) state that assessment approaches and instruments that are culturally appropriate and non-biased should be used in assessing young children. For many young children who are referred for evaluation, identifying appropriate and nonbiased instruments and strategies is a challenge. Most instruments which are norm-referenced (i.e., standardized) have not included children who are culturally and linguistically diverse in the norming population. These instruments cannot be used fairly, then, as a measure of development for children who differ from the norming population either culturally or linguistically. Yet using instruments which are not norm-referenced is not necessarily the solution to this problem. Most procedures for assessing young children rely on child development "milestones" taken from other tests or research (Bailey & Nabors, 1996); these milestones have typically been derived from studies involving only children from white, middle-class backgrounds and therefore also may be biased.

Assessment of young children from culturally and linguistically diverse populations cannot be "business as usual."

The assessment team will need to read the examiner's manual of any instrument very carefully to determine how appropriate an instrument is for a particular child. For example, some instruments have been translated into another language, however, only English speaking children are represented in the norms. A test that has been translated may reflect a particular dialect of language and culture that is not appropriate for the child being tested. For example, in the Latino population, there are both cultural and linguistic differences among Puerto Ricans, Cubans, Mexicans, and groups from South America. Furthermore, tests which have been written in another language and normed on a population of monolingual speakers of that language may not be appropriate for children who are bilingual or who are immersed in an English educational environment (Figueroa, 1989; Schiff-Myers, 1992). Frequently, those responsible for assessing a child for whom English is a second language find that typical instruments and procedures cannot be used and, in fact, there is no commercially available assessment instrument which is appropriate for use. Instead, the assessment team will need to design an assessment plan which is tailored to the child being evaluated.

In addition to the typical team of professionals and family members, it will be extremely helpful to have at least one other person on the assessment

team who speaks the child's language and is familiar with the child's culture, and at least one member who is experienced in bilingual education (Bondurant-Utz, 1994). For example, a school district in Wisconsin found increasing numbers of children of immigrant families from Eastern Europe referred for evaluation for special education. For these children, the school district changed the composition of the assigned assessment teams to include an individual

from the Eastern European community (hired as a Community Consultant) and also a teacher licensed in English as a second language (ESL). In this way, needed expertise was added to the assessment teams in order to plan and carry out an appropriate assessment.

It is recommended that the assessment plan include a variety of procedures including observation in school and home settings, interviews with family members and child care providers, and, of course, careful selection and use of assessment instruments. Following are strategies which might be helpful in devising the assessment plan:

- As discussed prior, assessment of language dominance and proficiency should be completed first in order to plan further assessment.
- Informal methods, such as observations, interviews of parents and caregivers, and play-based assessment in a comfortable, familiar setting should be used in addition to or in place of more formal methods (Santos de Barona & Barona, 1991).
- Any instrument that might be used should be examined for cultural bias by a person from the child's cultural group. Modifications can be made so items will be culturally appropriate. These modifications, however, will invalidate the scoring of the instrument. In this case, the test can be used as a descriptive measure rather than for reporting scores, and the team's decision will be based on informed clinical opinion rather than on test scores.

- Testing might be done by a professional who is from or very knowledgeable about the child's cultural group and who speaks the same language or dialect that is the child's primary language.
- If such a professional is not available, testing might be done with the assistance of an interpreter/translator or a cultural guide who works in conjunction with the assessment team in administering and interpreting assessments.
- Additional suggestions for planning and carrying out assessment of children for whom English is a second language are available in manuals developed by the state of Washington (Billings et al., 1997) and the state of Colorado (Moore & Beatty, 1995). Both of these products contain many helpful suggestions for assessment teams. To order Billings et al., call (360) 753-6733. To order Moore and Beatty, call (303) 492-3066.

Assessment of young children from culturally and linguistically diverse populations cannot be "business as usual." Considerable information from the child and family should be obtained and considered prior to the initial referral for assessment. The assessment team must then make every effort to tailor the assessment so it becomes appropriate for the individual child and family. Efforts to provide a culturally and linguistically appropriate assessment will help to guard against over- or underidentification of children for special education services.

Notes

You can reach Mary McLean by e-mail at mmclean@uwm.edu

The preparation of this manuscript was partially supported by the Early Childhood Research Institute on Culturally and Linguistically Appropriate Services (US Office of Education #H024560006).

References

Bailey, D., & Nabors, L. (1996). Tests and test development. In M. McLean, D. Bailey, & M. Wolery (Eds.), *Assessing infants and preschoolers with special needs* (pp. 24–45). Columbus, OH: Merrill.

Barrera, I. (1993). Effective and appropriate instruction for all children: The challenge of cultural/linguistic diversity and young children with special needs. *Topics in Early Childhood Special Education, 13*(4), 461–487.

Barrera Metz, I. (1991). Learning from personal experiences. In M. Anderson & P. Goldberg (Eds.), *Cultural competence in screening and assessment: Implications for services to young children with special needs ages birth through five.* Chapel Hill, NC: National Early Childhood Technical Assistance System.

Billings, J. A., Pearson, J., Gill, D. H., & Shureen, A. (1997). *Evaluation and assessment in early childhood special education.* Olympia, WA: Office of the Superintendent of Public Instruction.

Bondurant-Utz, J. (1994). Cultural diversity. In J. A. Bondurant-Utz & L.B. Luciano (Eds.), *A practical guide to infant and preschool assessment in special education* (pp. 73–98). Boston: Allyn & Bacon.

Children's Defense Fund. (1989). *A vision for America's future*. Washington, DC: Author.

Figueroa, R. A. (1989). Psychological testing of linguistic-minority students: Knowledge gaps and regulations. *Exceptional Children, 56*(2), 145–152.

Hakuta, K. (1986). *Mirror of language: The debate on bilingualism*. New York: Basic Books.

Kayser, H. (1989). Speech and language assessment of Spanish-English speaking children. *Language, Speech and Hearing Services in Schools, 20*, 226–244.

Kayser, H. (1993). Hispanic cultures. In D.E. Battle (Ed.), *Communication disorders in multicultural populations* (pp. 114–157). Boston: Andover Medical Publishers.

Langdon, H. W. (1989). Language disorder or difference? Assessing the language skills of Hispanic students. *Exceptional Children, 56*(2), 160–167.

Lund, N. J., & Duchan, J. F. (1993). *Assessing children's language in naturalistic contexts* (3rd ed.). Englewood Cliffs, NJ: Prentice Hall.

Mattes, L. J., & Omark, D. R. (1991). *Speech and language assessment for the bilingual handicapped* (2nd ed.). Oceanside, CA: Academic Communication Associates.

McCardle, P., Kim, J., Grube, C., & Randall, V. (1995). An approach to bilingualism in early intervention. *Infants and Young Children, 7*(3), 63–73.

Moore, S. M., & Beatty, J. (1995). *Developing cultural competence in early childhood assessment*. Boulder, CO: University of Colorado.

Neisworth, J., & Bagnato, S. (1996). Assessment. In S. Odom & M. McLean (Eds.), *Early intervention/Early childhood special education: Recommended practices* (pp. 23–58). Austin, TX: Pro-Ed.

Ortiz, A. (1984). Choosing the language of instruction for exceptional bilingual children. *Teaching Exceptional Children, 16*, 208–212.

Ortiz, A., & Maldonado-Colon, E. (1986). Recognizing learning disabilities in bilingual children: How to lessen inappropriate referrals of language minority students to special education. *Journal of Reading, Writing, and Learning Disabilities International*, pp. 43–56.

Roseberry-McKibben, C. (1994). Assessment and intervention for children with limited English proficiency and language disorders. *American Journal of Speech-Language Pathology, 3*(3), 77–88.

Santos de Barona, M., & Barona, A. (1991). The assessment of culturally and linguistically different preschoolers. *Early Childhood Research Quarterly, 6*, 363–376.

Schiff-Meyers, N. (1992). Considering arrested language development and language loss in the assessment of second language learners. *Language, Speech, and Hearing Services in Schools, 23*, 28–33.

Tabors, P. O. (1998). What early childhood educators need to know: Developing effective programs for linguistically and culturally diverse children and families. *Young Children 53*(6), 20–26.

Yansen, E., & Shulman, E. (1996). Language assessment: Multicultural considerations. In L. Suzuki, P. Meller, & J. Ponterotto (Eds.), *The handbook of multicultural assessment* (pp. 353–393). San Francisco: Jossey-Bass.

Children in Context

Portfolio Assessment in the Inclusive Early Childhood Classroom

Ellen M. Lynch, Ed.D., University of Cincinnati
Nancy A. Struewing, M.Ed., Winton Woods School District,
Cincinnati, OH

Assessment, or the systematic collection of information about a child (Wolery, 1994), is frequently an integral part of inclusive early childhood programs. Too often, however, teachers may not have a clear understanding of *what* or *why* they are assessing. Wolery (1994) has identified seven purposes for taking part in the information-gathering process: screening, making diagnoses, determining eligibility for special services, instructional planning, determining placement, monitoring progress, and evaluating programs. When teachers determine that they need information about a child for a specific reason, they can then decide upon the strategy to use to obtain that data. In this way, the purpose for assessing guides the data-gathering process (Cook, Tessier, & Klein, 2000).

Portfolio assessment is a strategy that can be used when teachers wish to collect data to inform the instructional planning process and to monitor a child's developmental progress. According to Meisels (1993), a portfolio is a " ... purposeful collection of children's work that illustrates their efforts, progress, and achievements" (p. 37). With this approach, teachers observe and record children's behavior, document activities, systematically collect work samples, reflect on the meaning of what they have observed, and then use the information for curriculum planning and change (MacDonald, 1997).

While portfolio assessment has been discussed recently as a valuable tool for classrooms with typically developing children (Gronlund, 1998; MacDonald, 1997; Shores & Grace, 1998), this strategy can be used quite successfully by teachers in inclusive environments as well. In the remainder of this article, we provide an overview of the benefits of using portfolio assessment for children with special needs followed by a discussion of the steps one might follow when implementing this strategy in an inclusive classroom.

Benefits of Portfolio Assessment

Portfolio assessment is particularly advantageous for teachers who wish to obtain data for purposes of instructional planning or to gather information about a child's developmental progress. Some of the specific benefits of this method include:

- *Observations and work samples are collected in a naturalistic setting.* This fact is particularly important because it is in such settings that children with special needs " ... will most likely demonstrate the knowledge, skills, and attitudes that truly represent their attainments" (Hills, 1993, p. 23). As a result, the monitoring and revision of instructional and IEP goals becomes a much more meaningful process due to the accuracy and richness of the data collected.
- *Data collection is ongoing and is integrated with curriculum planning.* As work samples are added to the portfolio, the progression of developmental change can be observed without waiting for a more formalized assessment. Progress toward IEP goals can be measured readily and curriculum adaptations can be made more quickly.
- *Data collection focuses on the whole child.* Teachers have the opportunity to document activities and successes that may not be part of the formal IEP. Parents and teachers may gain a more comprehensive view of the child's abilities.
- *Information is collected from many sources.* Many individuals can be involved in the process, providing a more accurate picture of a child's abilities. All members of the teaching team can make contributions representing a variety of perspectives.
- *The child has the opportunity to be an active participant in the process.* Children serve as members of the team. As they analyze their own work and make decisions about what to include, they may develop greater autonomy, decision-making skills, and self-esteem.
- *Inclusion of children from diverse backgrounds and with diverse abilities is supported.* Portfolios serve as a tremendous support to

true inclusion in that all children are involved in the process. Because this method allows teachers to track each child's progress individually, it works well for children representing diverse cultures and for those with diverse abilities. The fact that all children are included provides the added benefit of helping parents and teaching team members realize that each child is *truly* part of the community of learners.

First Things First: Preparation for Portfolio Assessment

There are several issues to be considered before beginning the actual process of data collection. Teachers who take the time to reflect on these issues maximize their potential for success with the portfolio assessment process:

- *Establish what it is that you hope to assess and why.* Are you interested in collecting data about social, emotional, physical, and/or cognitive development? Are you more concerned about specific IEP goals or about developmental progress in general? Do you plan to use the information for instructional planning and change? "Without a purpose, a portfolio is just a folder of student work" (Grace, 1992).
- *Determine how the portfolio process can be integrated into your overall assessment system.* For example, you may be required to complete standardized testing in your classroom. Consider how a variety of assessment strategies might support each other.
- *Start slowly.* If the use of portfolios is new for you, begin with a specific focus. You may find it helpful to develop a "contents checklist" outlining the data you hope to collect. During the first year, the portfolio will develop slowly as you assess and evaluate what is most important to you, the child, and the entire assessment process.
- *Research the possibilities.* There are several resources to help you determine which strategies seem to fit your teaching style as well as your particular group of children. (Many of these sources are listed in the References at the end of this article.)
- *Develop a process whereby confidentiality is maintained.* Consider how the portfolios will be presented in your classroom. Placing

them in the classroom on a movable storage shelf/cart enables parents and other professionals working with the children to be able to review the portfolios easily. At the end of the session, the entire cart can be moved into a locked room until the next day. (A friendly memo to parents that they should only look at their own child's portfolio is usually sufficient.)

• *Consider what will be kept and what will be given to the parent and child.* While not required, it is assumed that most materials placed in a portfolio are given to the parent at the end of the school year. However, if there is a child in your room who may be in your program for multiple years, you may decide to retain some items. Rather than keeping the original, it is preferable to duplicate the desired items. It is particularly helpful to keep a copy of any checklists and final summary reports. A small collection of work samples may also be kept.

• *Consider how you will encourage teaming.* Before the school year begins, you might conduct a brief training on the use of portfolios for those who will be interacting with the children on a regular basis: assistant teachers, therapists, student teachers, parents, classroom volunteers, etc. Distribute copies of forms and provide a sample portfolio for review. Also hold meetings with the contributors as part of the assessment process. Meeting on a regular schedule will help keep everyone current and the portfolio up to date.

After reflecting on these considerations, you are ready to begin. In the next section we offer specific suggestions about what information can be gathered and how the data might be stored and organized.

Nuts and Bolts of Information Gathering: What to Include and How

Gathering Information: What to Include

In general, the portfolio might include any "product" that would provide clues to a child's developmental progress and/or movement toward goals. *What* you collect should be determined by the actual purpose of your assessment. As a result, the following list should be considered suggestions rather than a definitive list:

... [T]he portfolio might include any "product" that would provide clues to a child's developmental progress and/or movement toward goals.

Figure 1: Sample Letter to Parents

Dear Parents,

I'm going to try something a little different this year and would like you to participate as much as you feel comfortable. I will be using "portfolios" this year for assessing and keeping track of each child's progress. I have done a lot of reading, thinking, and organizing, and would like to explain a little about this system and what to expect. Many items that I will keep in the portfolios reflect practices that teachers at our school have done for many years. The portfolios are just a more systematic and organized method of recording daily activities.

Each child's portfolio will be divided into four areas of development (language, cognitive, motor, and social-emotional), and goals will be listed for each area. In each area, there may be teacher anecdotes, your child's dictation, pictures/painting, work samples, photographs, etc. All these things will help document each child's interests, skills, and successes.

The portfolios will be stored in the classroom where parents and children will have access to them on a daily basis. The most beneficial portfolios are those that contain information from anyone who interacts with your child. Parent input is very important! If your child draws a picture, or dictates to you something that happened that day at school or at home, please ask your child if he or she would like to include it in his or her portfolio and send it to school with any comments.

I encourage you to come into the classroom at any time and take a few minutes with your child to look through his or her portfolio. One advantage of using portfolios is that each child's progress is compared only to his or her own, not other children's or to some arbitrary test score. I also ask that you please be respectful of other children's portfolios and do not look through them unless you have been invited to do so by a child's parents.

Another important part of the portfolios is the child's own impressions and comments about his or her work. Please feel free to jot down any comments made by your child as you look through his or her work, and attach these to the page. There will be a date stamp and "sticky notes" available near the portfolios for your use.

I would like each child to design the cover of his or her own portfolio. I will have paper and markers available to the children during the first few days of school. If your child would like to make his or her cover at home, that is okay too!

I'm looking forward to a really great year!

Sincerely,

Teacher

- *Letter to the parents.* Figure 1 includes a sample letter to parents describing the portfolio process. While we recommend sending this letter before school begins, a copy should be included in the portfolio itself.
- *Family information.* The information you collect from parent questionnaires and conversations can be very helpful for understanding their perceptions of their children, what their expectations are for the school year, and personal information about their children that can help guide your planning, or alert you to any other considerations. Moreover, knowing specific information such as pet names and sibling names can be very helpful when establishing an initial relationship with a child.
- *Parent comments.* Because parent involvement is strongly encouraged, include a form that parents can use to comment quickly on their child's progress. The form can be as simple as a piece of paper provided in the portfolio that has spaces for the parents to write and date their comments.
- *Conference notes.* Keep track of parent conferences: what was discussed, what concerns there may have been, or what goals may have been set. These notes are very helpful to use as a reference for future planning and/or follow-up, and will provide a place to

document shared strategies that may have been discussed to link home and school. Reviewing such notes also is helpful in preparing for the next conference.

- *Audio taped recordings.* These recordings are an effective way to assess the child's language development over time and may provide insight into personality traits of the child. (For in-depth analysis of audio tapes, you may wish to work with a speech/language therapist.) Allow children to listen to their tapes afterwards in case they want to add any additional comments.
- *Videotapes.* These recordings may help teachers and parents obtain a more complete picture of the child's development and interaction with the environment. Videotape is particularly useful when teachers wish to demonstrate progress that may be very difficult to document. For example, if an IEP goal related to feeding has been set, video recordings of a child feeding himself or herself in September, October, and November might show definitive, yet subtle, progress.
- *Activity checklist.* Knowing which activities are most- or least-often visited can be very important information. For example, if you observe that a child avoids all sensory activities, you may want to ask an occupational therapist for some activities that may help the child desensitize his or her skin and therefore allow him or her to enjoy these activities. If you notice a child avoiding the manipulatives and activities such as stringing, you may want to pursue this issue to rule out any fine motor delays. A child who avoids the music area or the listening area may have auditory concerns. You can develop a brief checklist or chart that lists the children's names and the activities available in your room. Regular completion of the chart provides an indication of each child's interests and movement throughout the classroom.

In some preschool classrooms, children regularly write in their own journals.

- *Work samples.* These are critical in assessing the child's progress. Some samples you may want to collect are: writing, painting, cutting activities, collages, math activities, drawings, log of books read to (by) the child, class charts/graphs experienced by the child, child dictations, and quotations. Note that many of these can be recorded with a photograph if the actual sample is not used.
- *Journal pages.* In some preschool classrooms, children regularly write in their own journals. These pages provide insight into the children's developing writing skills and cognitive processes.

Children will write about and draw things that are important to them, and this can be important information to document. Photocopies of the pages can be used as well. (A child with a disability, while participating in the same activity as the rest of the children, may require special modifications for holding the pencil or touch and visual cues to be more successful. You may wish to consult with an occupational therapist.)

- *Group projects.* Photograph children working together, record their comments, and make a photocopy for each child involved. Topics may include language experience stories about field trips, visitors, special group time activities, cooking experiences, or special school events.

- *Photographs.* A photograph of a child involved in an activity, in combination with teacher notes and child comments, allows you to assess many skills at one time. For example, if your focus is on the development of a child's maturing pattern of grasping, you might include photographs, taken over a period of time, that show the child moving from a whole-hand grasp to a pincer grasp. It should be noted that digital cameras, while expensive, could be extremely valuable tools in the classroom. With them, teachers are able to see immediately if the pictures they have taken capture the behavior they wish to document. Additionally, color pictures can be printed immediately and added to the portfolio with no waiting for developing.

A photograph of a child involved in an activity, in combination with teacher notes and child comments, allows you to assess many skills at one time.

Photographs are extremely beneficial when used with children who cannot or choose not to produce products to take home or put in the portfolio. Children with severe disabilities might be included in this group. Photos of block structures, group projects, and interactions with other children help to provide permanent reminders. Equally important is the fact that parents have the opportunity to see their child as an active, included part of the classroom.

When organizing photographs, it is particularly helpful to mount each photo on an 8½ x 11 sheet of paper that has several lines drawn across the bottom for text. Duplicate these photo sheets in large volume so they are readily available for the teacher to make notes or for children to write or dictate comments about what is happening in the photo. It is also very helpful to have a

Brailler available to enable children with visual impairments to read the text that is written.

- *Anecdotal records.* Anecdotal records are brief, factual, and nonjudgmental notes that a teacher makes about a child's behavior. They record activities, events, and how the child interacts with his or her surroundings (MacDonald, 1997; Shores & Grace, 1998). Anecdotal records provide the opportunity to record information about a child's process rather than a final product that has been generated.

While anecdotes can be written on index cards or small sheets of paper, a form developed specifically for classroom use can also be quite effective (see Figure 2). The form helps to organize thinking and helps guide the teacher in making comments that are more specific and objective.

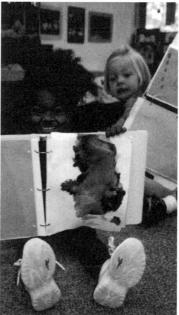

Additionally, this tool provides a mechanism by which many individuals, even those not familiar with anecdote writing, can contribute to the assessment process thereby providing a more comprehensive picture of the child's abilities and interests. (Note that "Goal" is included in the "Area" section of the sample form shown in Figure 2. This entry would be used to identify an anecdote that relates to a specific IEP goal while at the same time maintaining confidentiality.)

Gathering Information: Organization

Now that you have considered your purpose(s) for assessing, and have determined what materials to include in the portfolio, you must consider just how the information will be stored and organized. There are several ways to store the portfolio information, such as binders, X-ray folders, file folders, pizza boxes, shoeboxes, or drawers. When developing your organizational system, consider the following:

- *It must be possible to divide containers into sections.* The sections of your portfolio will be determined by the purpose(s) of your assessment process. In the example, the contents of the portfolio are divided into sections representing four developmental

Figure 2: Sample Anecdotal Record Form

Name of Child: *Kaitlyn*

Date: *August 26*   Ⓜ T W TH F

Art	Blocks	Books	Computer
Dramatic Play	Group Time	Lunch	Manipulatives
(Math)	Muscle room	Music	Nap
Outside	Puzzles	Science	Sensory Table
Snack	Special Activity	Writing Center	

Area: (Cognitive)   Motor   Language
          Social-Emotional   Goal

With: Peer   (Teacher)   Other Adult
          Self   Sm. Group   Lg. Group

Played bus grid game—could group sets of 3 and could take
correct # of covers; recognized the blank space on the dice as being
"nothing"

Initials: *NAS*

domains: language, cognitive, motor, and social-emotional. The first page of each section is a sheet providing descriptors that characterize the particular domain (see the sample in Figure 3). These dividers supply information for those who may be providing documentation (teachers; student teachers; parents; occupational, physical, and speech and language therapists; etc.). The various goal(s) identified within each domain can be adjusted or removed to meet the particular developmental needs and interests of each group of children. Portfolios can also be divided by time periods-quarters, semesters, months, etc. (Note: Divider pages with tabs and plastic

Figure 3: Sample Developmental Domain Descriptor Sheet

Language Domain

Developmental Goal 1: Children will develop their abilities to use all forms of communication: verbal, nonverbal, written, and spoken, for a variety of purposes and situations.

Developmental Expectations:

1. Children can make sense of the variety of print that they read, write, and observe:

   a. Recognize own name in print

   b. Recognize other children's names in print

   c. Explore uses of print

   d. Understand the relationship between spoken word and written word

   e. Experiment with sound-symbol relationships

   f. Use writing implement in a purposeful way

   g. Begin to understand conventions of book reading (read from front to back, book held right-side up)

   h. Join in reading familiar words and phrases

2. Children can make sense of the variety of messages to which they listen:

   a. Follow classroom routines

   b. Follow one- and two-step directions

3. Children can speak using appropriate forms, conventions, and styles to communicate ideas and information to different audiences for different purposes:

   a. Retell stories

   b. Verbally share ideas, stories, and events

   c. Initiate conversations

   d. Formulate/ask questions

   e. Use language to attempt to problem solve conflict situations

   f. Use appropriate vocal quality and intensity

   g. Use appropriate fluency, rate, and inflection

   h. Dictate stories to adults

   i. Speak in complete sentences

4. Children can use computers to facilitate communication:

   a. Experiment with developmentally appropriate software

   b. Use keyboards, touch pads, and mouse controller in developmentally appropriate ways

   c. Explore transferring thoughts and ideas into print using the computer

page protectors may be included, as appropriate, to keep the contents of the portfolio organized.)

- *The system must be easily accessible to both the teacher and the children*. Have a place in your room to put forms, markers, a hole punch, plastic bags (for audio tapes), and any other supplies you will need. It helps to also have a box for those papers that cannot be added to the portfolio immediately. After class each day, take a few minutes to add these to individual portfolios. It can be very overwhelming if things start to pile up and you get behind!
- *The portfolios should take up as little space as possible, yet they need to be big enough to store an entire year's worth of work*. For three-dimensional projects, artwork, or building structures that are too big to fit in the portfolio, take a photograph and store that instead.
- *The portfolios should be inexpensive*. To help defray costs, you may want to ask each child to bring in a binder at the beginning of each school year. Moreover, you could request that each parent bring in a roll of film once or twice per year. (We encourage you to watch the newspaper for "free double prints" promotions if you wish to keep pictures for your personal use.) If parents ask for suggestions for classroom donations or ideas for teacher gifts, ask for film!

> *... You could request that each parent bring in a roll of film once or twice per year.*

A final note about portfolio assessment: No matter how you choose to collect and store the information, be patient. Try to utilize the same system for at least one school year before deciding to change. Making major modifications in midstream can be confusing to both children and adults. Additionally, using a particular system throughout the year will provide adequate time to evaluate the changes you might like to introduce in the future.

Completing the Assessment Circle: Reflection, Discussion, and Change

This article has provided considerable information about collecting information and documenting experience. However, portfolio assessment requires that the resulting data be used to inform the instructional planning process. "Teachers must reflect on *what* they have observed and recorded in relation to program goals and objectives for each child" (Hills, 1993, p. 27). The data collected must be used to plan and revise

Teachers must reflect on what they have observed and recorded in relation to program goals and objectives for each child ....

the curriculum as well as to establish new goals for *all* children in the classroom (Gronlund, 1998; Meisels, 1993). All those who work with the children must systematically study and discuss the contents of the portfolio to determine what patterns of behavior have been observed and the changes, if any, that must occur within the classroom. Some suggestions for completing the assessment process include:

- *Schedule formal meetings.* Because classrooms are such busy places, regularly scheduled meetings should be held for the specific purpose of reviewing portfolio contents, developing new plans, and establishing new goals.
- *Arrange for the appropriate equipment.* Make sure you arrange to have a VCR with monitor and/or audio tape player when viewing or listening to tapes.
- *Determine the agenda ahead of time and remind participants.* Teaming is a critical aspect of portfolio assessment and organization is necessary to maximize the possibility for success. When conferencing about a child with multiple concerns, you may choose to focus on only one or two developmental domains at each meeting.
- *Complete each meeting with a plan for further documentation and action.* Determine the "holes" in the data that have been collected. Has there been progress toward IEP goals? If not, what activities should be added or changed? What will be the focus of discussion for next month's meeting?
- *Stay focused on the child.* While portfolios can provide teachers with invaluable information about children, their interests, and abilities, there is one word of caution. When beginning the process it can become quite consuming, and it is quite easy to become focused on the product (i.e., the portfolio and its contents). Certainly, having aesthetically appealing, neatly organized portfolios is pedagogically sound and shows respect for the children. However, the real focus of your efforts should be on process-documenting a child's developmental progress over time. Katz and Chard (1996) assert that when focusing on a final product, it is easy to miss the important "false starts and persistent efforts" that a child may demonstrate on his or her way to a product. It is critical to the success of the portfolio system that the teacher maintain a focus on how the *child* is changing, *not* the portfolio.

While the portfolio assessment process requires significant planning, organization, and perseverance, the benefits realized are well worth the effort. Teachers are able to collect significant information about children's interests and developmental levels that can, in turn, impact further curriculum planning and implementation. Additionally, teachers have the opportunity to come to know the children in their classrooms on a much deeper level.

Note
You can reach Ellen M. Lynch by e-mail at ellen.lynch@uc.edu

References
Cook, R. E., Tessier, A., & Klein, M. D. (2000). *Adapting early childhood curricula for children in inclusive settings*. Englewood Cliffs, NJ: Merrill.

Grace, C. (1992). *The portfolio and its use: Developmentally appropriate assessment of young children.* (ERIC Digest No. EDO-PS-92-11.)

Gronlund, G. (1998). Portfolios as an assessment tool: Is collection of work enough? *Young Children, 53*(3), 4–10.

Hills, T. W. (1993). Assessment in context—Teachers and children at work. *Young Children, 48*(5), 20–28.

Katz, L. G., & Chard, S. C. (1996). *The contribution of documentation to the quality of early childhood education.* Available online: http://ericeece.org/pubs/digests/1996/lkchar96.html.

MacDonald, S. (1997). *The portfolio and its use: A road map for assessment*. Little Rock, AR: Southern Early Childhood Association.

Meisels, S. J. (1993). Remaking classroom assessment with the work sampling system. *Young Children, 48*(5), 34–40.

Shores, E. F., & Grace, C. (1998). *The portfolio book: A step-by-step guide for teachers*. Beltsville, MD: Gryphon House.

Wolery, M. (1994). Assessing children with special needs. In M. Wolery & J. S. Wilbers (Eds.), *Including children with special needs in early childhood programs* (pp. 71–96). Washington, DC: National Association for the Education of Young Children (NAEYC).

Easing the Transition to Kindergarten

Assessment of Social, Behavioral, and Functional Skills in Young Children With Disabilities

Beth Rous, Ed.D., University of Kentucky
Rena A. Hallam, Ph.D., University of Kentucky

"Okay boys and girls, it's time to sit down now."

"Let's all get our coats on and get ready to

go outside to the playground."

"Get in line. It's time to go to lunch."

"Please finish your work and put your things away."

One of the unchangeable processes in the education of our children is the need to move children between and among various programs. As children move from preschool programs to school-age programs, the expectations of teachers change. Children are expected to work more independently, follow group directions, and attend to their own needs. The transition from an early childhood environment to a school setting can be extremely stressful to families (Fowler, Chandler, Johnson, & Stella, 1988; Healy, Keesee, & Smith, 1989). In an effort to alleviate this stress, preparing the child and family for these changes can help make the process more successful for everyone involved (Hains, 1992; Rous, Hemmeter, & Schuster, 1994; Vincent, 1992).

Transition has been defined by many in the fields of early childhood and early childhood special education (Hains, Fowler, & Chandler, 1988; Huntinger, 1981; Wolery, 1989). Lombardi (1992) defines transition as differences in services among environments, agencies, or institutions. Kagan (1992) further describes transitions as horizontal, movement across environments within the same time frame, and vertical, movement across environments across time.

In an effort to ease the transition process for children with disabilities, the preparation of children and families for the next programmatic environment has become an important component of program planning. Research has been conducted to explore the expectations of teachers in inclusive settings in an effort to better prepare children for such environments. This work has demonstrated that teachers in general education classrooms and child care centers focus more on social, behavioral, and functional skill areas (e.g., cooperative and nonaggressive behavior, caring for bathroom needs) than academic areas (e.g., counting, naming letters) (Hains, Fowler, Schwartz, Kottwitz, & Rosenkoetter, 1989; Hemmeter & Rous, 1998; Johnson, Gallagher, Cook, & Wong, 1995; Murphy & Vincent, 1989). These research findings have prompted an increased emphasis on supporting social, behavioral, and functional skills in preschool children with disabilities.

Developmentally Appropriate Practice

The obvious challenge in examining functional, social, and behavioral skills in young children with disabilities is the assessment of such skills in light of appropriate developmental expectations. Professional recommendations for developmentally appropriate practice for children with and without disabilities highlight the need for early childhood programming based upon child development research, individual needs of children, and the needs and values of families and communities (Bredekamp & Copple, 1997). Given a developmentally appropriate context, it is possible to assess children's skills in these areas without imposing inappropriate expectations on young children.

[Research] has demonstrated that teachers in general education classrooms and child care centers focus more on social, behavioral, and functional skills areas ... than academic areas.

The role of the teacher (or the person who is completing the assessment) is critical in this process. The teacher must consider the age of the child, the child's individual needs, and the needs of the child's family when examining social and behavioral skills. Thus, a four-year old child should not be expected to follow a long series of directions or wait in line for ten minutes in an effort to prepare him or her for kindergarten. However, one can determine the status of the child's ability to follow simple directions and wait for brief periods for an upcoming activity.

This process must take into consideration the relationship of the cultural and social practices of the community. All of this information can be helpful for teachers and parents in preparing the child for the next setting as well as adapting the next setting to meet the needs of the child.

Development of the Helpful Entry Level Skills Checklist

The Helpful Entry Level Skills Checklist (Byrd & Rous, 1990) was designed to assist teachers in selecting skills that would facilitate the transition of children from preschool into public school kindergarten and school-age programs. The instrument is a tool that can be used to assess the functional, social, and behavioral skills of children between three and six years of age. Sample items are listed in Figure 1. The skills included on the checklist are those which have been identified as important to the success of children transitioning into inclusive kindergarten and school-age settings (Hains et al., 1989; Hemmeter & Rous, 1997; Johnson et al., 1995).

The Helpful Entry Level Skills (HELS) Checklist was originally designed in 1985 (and revised in 1990) as part of a model demonstration project funded through the U.S. Department of Education, Handicapped Children's Early Education Program (HCEEP). Kindergarten, preschool, first grade, and special education teachers were asked to identify skills helpful for children entering the public school program. This listing of skills was then compared with the current literature on skill expectations and sent to a panel of outside reviewers.

Based upon their input, skills included on the checklist and formatting of the assessment tool were revised. The checklist was then field tested with teachers in preschool programs across the community for 31 children. Data were collected on the helpfulness of the assessment tool on facilitating transition planning for these children, including follow-up once children transitioned into school-age programs. This follow-up indicated 68% of teachers in school-age programs believed the Helpful Entry Level Skills Checklist provided realistic information about the child's skill levels which assisted in the adjustment of the child to the school-age setting (Wolery & Stilwell, 1986).

Figure 1: Helpful Entry Level Skills (HELS) Checklist Samples

Child's Name _____

Person(s) Completing Form _____

Skill	Pretest Date			Midyear Date			Posttest Date			Comments
	Yes	No	I/E	Yes	No	I/E	Yes	No	I/E	
Work Skills										
1. Refrains from disturbing the activities of others.										
2. Stops activity when given direction to "Stop."										
3. Works independently on developmentally appropriate material.										
4. Completes task when given developmentally appropriate material.										
5. Follows simple directions related to task.										
6. Engages in developmentally appropriate activities for 1-3-10-15 minutes.										
7. Waits until directions are completed to begin activity.										

Target Skills # (s) _____

Key: V = Verbal Prompt/Guidance   P = Physical Prompt/Guidance
      M = Model Prompt/Guidance   I/E = Inconsistent or Emergent

Byrd, M. R., & Rous, B. S. (1990). *Helpful Entry Level Skills Checklist* (Rev. ed.). Lexington, KY: Child Development Centers of the Bluegrass, Inc.

Since the initial development of the instrument, it has been reviewed and refined to reflect current research on skills identified as critical to successful transitions (e.g., Fowler, 1980; Hemmeter & Rous, 1998; Vincent, Salisbury, et al., 1980). The resulting checklist includes social, behavioral, and functional skills such as following directions, turn taking, following class routines and rules, and independent functioning.

In an effort to help teachers assess social and behavioral skills in a developmentally appropriate manner, interpretation guidelines by children's ages have been developed for each skill item on the HELS Checklist. Table 1 provides an example of several skills found on the HELS Checklist and how it is to be interpreted for young children of varying ages. Items must be considered differently for children of varying ages in order to account for developmental differences.

The acquisition of entry-level skills certainly is not and should not be a requirement for placement in any public school program, however it is hoped these types of skills can help children in their adjustment to new environments and facilitate their placement in the least restrictive environment. While it was not possible to determine a specific set of functional skills appropriate for all preschool children, it is possible to determine those skills that are common and desirable in most programs. The skills selected were seen as the most critical for facilitating children's successful transition from preschool to public school programs.

Using the HELS

The HELS Checklist offers a systematic way of recording and identifying specific functional skills for children going through the transition process. Once the checklist is administered and skills are identified, transition objectives can be identified and incorporated in the IFSP or IEP. The purpose for including objectives on the child's IFSP or IEP is to identify, with family members, issues and concerns related to the transition process. In addition to the entry-level skills, other areas in which families could be actively involved in their child's transition should be identified.

The HELS Checklist includes skills in five areas: classroom rules, work skills, communication, social/ behavioral, and self-management. The form includes a summary page, where demographic information is

Table 1: Helpful Entry Level Skills Checklist Developmental Ages

Skill	3 Years of Age	4 Years of Age	5 Years of Age	6 Years of Age
Communication				
#1 Comes to adult when signaled.	The child may need a verbal and physical prompt.	The child should come when signaled without an additional prompt.	The child should come when signaled without an additional prompt.	The child should come when signaled without an additional prompt.
#2 Communicates own needs and preferences.	The child may be able to communicate need or preference through a combination of verbal and nonverbal means when asked to do so. The child may not initiate communication about needs and preferences.	The child may be able to indicate needs and preferences verbally in response to adult prompts. The child may initiate communication about needs and preferences through nonverbal and verbal means.	The child may be able to communicate needs and preferences verbally in response to adult prompts. The child may initiate communication about needs and preferences verbally and nonverbally.	The child should be able to initiate or respond to adult prompts regarding needs and preferences using verbal and nonverbal means of communicating.
#3 Answers questions about self, family, name, address, age, birthdate, parents' names.	The child should know name and age.	The child should know name, age, parents' and siblings' names.	The child should know name, age, parents' and siblings' names.	The child should know all the listed information.
#4 Attends to peer or adult who is talking to group.	The child should be able to attend to peer or adult for short periods of time (five minutes) in the absence of distracting events in the classroom.	The child should be able to attend to peer or adult for short periods of time (five to ten minutes) with minimal distractions in the classroom.	The child should be able to attend to peer or adult for up to 15 minutes with minimal distractions in the classroom.	The child should be able to attend to adult or peer even in the presence of distractions.

Hemmeter, M. L., & Rous, B. S. (1992). *Developmental ages for skills included in the Helpful Entry Level Skills Checklist.* Lexington, KY: Child Development Centers of the Bluegrass, Inc.

Figure 2: Transition Skills Classroom Matrix

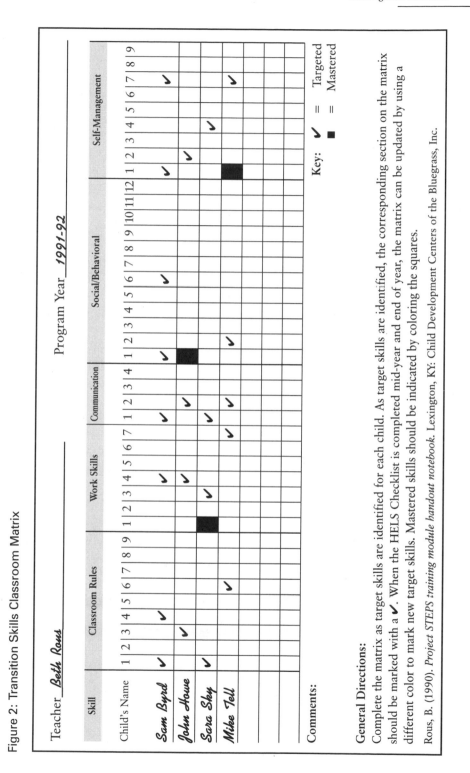

Teacher __Beth Rous__

Program Year __1991-92__

Key: ✔ = Targeted
      ■ = Mastered

General Directions:

Complete the matrix as target skills are identified for each child. As target skills are identified, the corresponding section on the matrix should be marked with a ✔. When the HELS Checklist is completed mid-year and end of year, the matrix can be updated by using a different color to mark new target skills. Mastered skills should be indicated by coloring the squares.

Rous, B. (1990). *Project STEPS training module handout notebook.* Lexington, KY: Child Development Centers of the Bluegrass, Inc.

listed and skills targeted for intervention are summarized. In addition, the form includes a general comment section and individual comment sections within each of the skill areas covered. A skill summary page and Classroom Matrix (see Figure 2) are included with each checklist. This skills summary page can be used to summarize skills targeted for intervention by highlighting targeted skills and sharing this information with families, related service personnel, and persons involved in the child's life (e.g., child care, extended family members). The Classroom Matrix is used to help teachers organize daily and weekly lessons and activities around needed skills for the children. In addition, the matrix can be used to assist with monitoring and documentation of skill development.

Since the intent of the checklist is to assist children with transition at ages five and six, many of the skills listed on the checklist are not programmatically appropriate for three-year old children. However, because many children who are experiencing developmental delays  may need to spend more time acquiring skills, teachers may begin planning for transition early by introducing key terminology children will need to understand at age five and six (e.g., line, row). In addition, assessing for entry level skills early allows opportunities to document supports used throughout the preschool program to assist children with social, behavioral, and functional skill development. For example, a child might need complete physical support (hand over hand) to care for bathroom needs at age three. However, by age four, the child might need only verbal support (e.g., "Remember to flush"). The specific types of support provided over time allows the current and future teachers to better plan for acquisition of new skills.

The HELS Checklist should be completed immediately prior to (i.e., by early intervention personnel) or within four to six weeks after the enrollment of a child in a preschool program. During the first few weeks of enrollment, the teacher should observe the child to determine the presence/absence of stated skills. The instrument is designed to be used as a checklist, not a formal assessment. Family members and other staff members who work with the child are encouraged to assist with completion of the checklist.

Guidelines for administering the checklist allow for three possible responses as well as notes for adaptations and clarifications (see Figure 1). The three responses are as follows:

1. Yes—The behavior is well-established. The child performs the skill independently or with only occasional support from staff. Within the "Yes" column, the skill may also be coded to indicate the level of prompt or support the child needs to perform the skill. A "V" is used to indicate that the child needs verbal support to accomplish the skill. Specific verbal cues should be recorded in the comment section. An "M" is used to indicate that the child needs modeling to accomplish the skill. Specific information on the type of model and from whom the model is provided (i.e., peer or staff) should be noted in the comment section. A "P" is used to indicate a need for physical support. Specific information on the type of physical support (e.g., hand over hand) should be noted in the comment section.

2. No—The behavior has not been observed or cannot be elicited even with supports.

3. I/E—The skill is inconsistent or emerging. For skills coded as inconsistent, the child exhibits the behavior only on occasion or the child has not generalized the skill across relevant environments. For skills coded as emergent, the child has demonstrated increased proficiency over the observation period without specific intervention from staff.

The comments section is provided for staff to indicate adaptations, supports, concerns, and/or reasons why the child might not exhibit the skill. For example, when assessing Communication skill #2 (communicates own needs and preferences) a nonverbal child may be able to indicate his or her needs by signing or using an augmentative communication system. In this case, the skill would be marked "Yes" and the comments section would be used to indicate how the child was able to communicate. The comments section becomes an important part of the assessment process because it provides clues about how to program for the child. For example, one might note after completing the checklist that the child is very responsive to two-word verbal reminders. This information should become part of the program plan for the child.

The comments section [on the HELS Checklist] is provided for staff to indicate adaptations, supports, concerns, and/or reasons why the child might not exhibit the skill.

After completing the checklist, those skills most likely to interfere with the child's successful transition should be identified. These skills are often naturally incorporated into the preschool curriculum, so skills targeted should be indicative of areas in which the child may need additional assistance or skills that are most critical for the child (e.g., safety issues). Information from the HELS Checklist can provide valuable information for joint planning efforts among families and professionals. As always, recommendations for families should respect family routines, schedules, and culture. Targeted skills also should be shared with other child care providers and related service personnel, to ensure consistency across environments.

The skills targeted for children will differ based upon their ages. For example, a child who is three years old may only be expected to perform certain skills with physical or verbal supports. Therefore program planning might revolve around introducing key terminology or in targeting skills which are prerequisite to other skills.

The checklist provides an opportunity for staff to reassess children's entry-level skills at mid-year. This allows staff a formalized mechanism for determining progress in targeted areas and to update targeted skills and goals for children. The staff would administer the posttest during the last month of school or when children are ready to leave a program. The same guidelines for completing the pretest should be followed during mid-year and posttesting. Staff are encouraged to use different colors to complete the checklist depending upon whether it is pre-, mid-, or post-. The form itself will reflect progress and a summary of progress should be included in any final reports or progress reports written by staff. During the final family conference, the checklist can be reviewed and suggestions for summer can be provided.

Follow-Up

It is suggested that, with parental permission, a copy of the HELS Checklist should be sent to the child's receiving teacher. This may be included in a follow-up packet prepared by the preschool. Educational summaries and reports, work samples, and other pertinent information also should be included. The child's family may deliver the packet to the receiving teacher or the preschool can send the packet through the school system.

Case Study

Mary is a four-year old girl enrolled in a preschool program which provides educational services for children with and without disabilities. Therapy services are provided based upon Mary's individualized education program (IEP). She has been diagnosed as having pervasive developmental disabilities and is currently receiving education, occupational therapy, and speech/language services. Current evaluation information shows areas of strength for Mary include her interest in computers, gross motor skills, a tendency to be routine-oriented, and her ability to nonverbally communicate likes and dislikes. Areas of need include expressive communication, social interactions, sensory motor processing, and fine motor skills. Mary has been referred to the public school system and will be entering a kindergarten classroom in the fall.

Mary will be leaving the preschool program at the end of the school year, and due to her lack of expressive communication skills, the teacher and occupational therapist decided to use the HELS Checklist to facilitate programming and to identify areas that would be the focus of transition planning. The pretest section of the checklist (see Figure 1) was completed in September by a team which included the occupational therapist, lead teacher, and Mary's mother, Tonya. After completion of the checklist, the team found Mary was able to accomplish many of the skills on the checklist with verbal supports. However, physical supports were still needed for her to accomplish many skills that involved in-class and in-school transitions.

After completion of the pretest, 12 skills were targeted for intervention for the school year. Of the 12 skills chosen, the four skill areas which were the highest priority were integrated into objectives for Mary's IEP. The other skills would be taught in conjunction with other activities within the normal routines and activities in the classroom. Skills targeted on Mary's IEP include: sits or waits appropriately, makes transitions between activities, stays with group outside the classroom, and separates from parents and accepts school.

Given the skills targeted for intervention and because Mary has a difficult time with in-class and in-school transitions, the following recommendations for the classroom were made. The occupational therapist and speech/language therapist developed a series of sequence cards made from Polaroid pictures to cue Mary during transitions between daily activities and for specific steps within each activity. For example, during circle, pictures included the calendar, weather chart, then the sink (indicating it was time to wash her hands for snack). Sequencing cards also were provided to the family for use at home.

In January, the occupational therapist and lead teacher completed the mid-test section of the checklist. Based upon the results, progress had been made in separating from parents and accepting school personnel. A new target skill was added to Mary's IEP: uses appropriate behavior to get staff attention. Information gained through the assessment was shared with Mary's mother, then public school personnel after the referral had been initiated.

In May, the posttest section of the checklist was completed. Of the original 12 skills targeted for direct or indirect intervention, five skills had been mastered. Progress or mastery had been made on a total of 37 of the 41 skills included on the checklist. Copies of the checklist and target skills were included in a follow-up packet that was sent to the school where Mary will be placed in the fall.

Mary will attend the summer camp program at the preschool, so targeted skills will be included on the program plan for summer. Recommendations for continuing intervention on targeted skills at home over the summer were provided at the family's request. These recommendations included the continued use of sequence cards at home, and a list of recommended toys that would help increase attending and turn taking skills and

The comments section [on the HELS Checklist] is provided for staff to indicate adaptations, supports, concerns, and/or reasons why the child might not exhibit the skill.

improve fine motor manipulation. The occupational therapist will continue to see Mary over the summer on a private basis, focusing on target skills in the summer therapy plan.

Collaborative Planning

The Helpful Entry Level Skills Checklist provides a systematic format for assessing and facilitating social, behavioral, and functional skills for preschool children. The format of the assessment is designed to allow for collaborative planning among families, teachers, paraprofessionals, and related service personnel. This tool holds promise of facilitating the transition process for young children and their families.

Notes

You can reach Beth Rous by e-mail at brous@uky.edu

Preparation for this manuscript was supported in part by Grant #H024D20027 and Grant #H024D6001 from the U.S. Department of Education, Early Education Programs for Children with Disabilities.

References

Bredekamp, S., & Copple, C. (1997). *Developmentally appropriate practice in early childhood programs: Revised edition.* Washington, DC: National Association for the Education of Young Children.

Byrd, M. R., & Rous, B. S. (1990). *Helpful Entry Level Skills Checklist* (Rev. ed.). Lexington, KY: Child Development Centers of the Bluegrass, Inc.

Fowler, S. A. (1980). Transition to public school. In K.E. Allen (Ed.), *Mainstreaming in early childhood education* (pp. 242–254). Albany, NY: Delmar Publications.

Fowler, S. A., Chandler, L. K., Johnson, T. E., & Stella, M. E. (1988). Individualized family involvement in school transitions: Gathering information and choosing the next program. *Journal of the Division of Early Childhood, 12*(3), 208–216.

Hains, A. H. (1992). Strategies for preparing preschool children with special needs for the kindergarten mainstream. *Journal of Early Intervention, 16*(4), 1–12.

Hains, A. H., Fowler, S. A., & Chandler, L. K. (1988). Planning school transitions: Family and professional collaboration. *Journal of the Division of Early Childhood, 12*(2), 108–115.

Hains, A. H., Fowler, S. A., Schwartz, I. S., Kottwitz, E., & Rosenkoetter, S. (1989). A comparison of preschool and kindergarten teacher expectations for school readiness. *Early Childhood Research Quarterly, 4*, 75–88.

Healy, A., Keesee, P. D., & Smith, B. S. (1989). *Early services for children with special needs: Transactions for family support.* Baltimore: Paul H. Brookes.

Hemmeter, M. L., & Rous, B. S. (1992). *Developmental ages for skills included in the Helpful Entry Level Skills Checklist.* Lexington, KY: Child Development Centers of the Bluegrass, Inc.

Hemmeter, M. L., & Rous, B. S. (1998). *Teachers' expectations of children transitioning into kindergarten or ungraded primary programs: A national survey.* Manuscript in progress.

Huntinger, P. L. (1981). Transition practices for handicapped young children: What experts say. *Journal of the Division of Early Childhood, 2*, 8–14.

Johnson, L. J., Gallagher, R. J., Cook, M. J., & Wong, P. (1995). Critical skills for kindergartners: Perceptions from kindergarten teachers. *Journal of Early Intervention, 19*(4), 315–327.

Kagan, S. (1992). The strategic importance of linkages and the transition between early childhood programs and early elementary school. In *Sticking together: Strengthening linkages and the transition between early childhood education and early elementary school* (Summary of a National Policy Forum). Washington, DC: U.S. Department of Education.

Lombardi, J. (1992). Beyond transition: Ensuring continuity in early childhood services. *ERIC Digest.* ERIC Clearinghouse on Elementary and Early Childhood Education. EPO-PS-92-3.

Murphy, M., & Vincent, L. J. (1989). Identification of critical skills for success in day care. *Journal of Early Intervention, 13*(3), 221–229.

Rous, B. (1990). *Project STEPS training module handout notebook.* Lexington, KY: Child Development Centers of the Bluegrass, Inc.

Rous, B., Hemmeter, M. L., & Schuster, J. (1994). Sequenced transition to education in the public schools: A systems approach to transition planning. *Topics in Early Childhood Special Education, 14*(3), 374–393.

Vincent, L. J. (1992). Families and early intervention: Diversity and competence. *Journal of Early Intervention, 16,* 166–172.

Vincent, L. J., Salisbury, C., Walter, G., Brown, P., Gruenewald, L., & Powers, M. (1980). Program evaluation and curricular development in early childhood special education: Criterion of the next environment. In W. Sailor, B. Wilcox, & L. Brown (Eds.), *Methods of instruction for severely handicapped students* (pp. 303–328). Baltimore: Paul H. Brookes.

Wolery, M. (1989). Transitions in early childhood special education: Issues and procedures. *Focus on Exceptional Children, 22*(2), 1–6.

Wolery, M., & Stilwell, D. (1986). *Formative evaluation study of Project steps: Year II evaluation 2.* Lexington, KY: University of Kentucky.

Resources
Within Reason
Assessment

Here you'll find additional resources to support the effective gathering, sharing, and use of information about infants, toddlers, and young children and their families. These resources range in price. Many are within an individual's budget while others may be more suitable for acquisition by an agency or school.

Camille Catlett, M.A., University of North Carolina at Chapel Hill

Books

Alternative Approaches to Assessing Young Children
by A. Losardo & A. Notari-Syverson (2001)

Six alternative assessment methods for young children (naturalistic, focused, performance, portfolio, dynamic, curriculum-based language) are detailed in this book. Chapters offer thorough descriptions of each approach, along with summaries of advantages and limitations, guidelines for implementation, suggestions for use in inclusive environments, and samples of data collection forms. A companion Web site (http://textbooks.brookespublishing.com/losardo) offers additional resources for faculty members who want to incorporate ideas from this book in their teaching (e.g., learning objectives, discussion strategies, self-study exams, PowerPoint slides, links to additional resources).

Paul H. Brookes Publishing
P.O. Box 10624
Baltimore, MD 21285-0624
(800) 638-3775
FAX (410) 337-8539
http://www.pbrookes.com

Assessing and Fostering the Development of a First and a Second Language in an Early Childhood Child Development Division
by the California Department of Education (1998)

This resource is designed to help train students, staff, and parents to assess and foster language development in young children from culturally and linguistically diverse backgrounds. Within the context of a preschool program, team members demonstrate and describe a six-step sequence through which they gather information, engage the participation of family members, and adjust the curriculum to support young language learners. A companion videotape, *Observing Preschoolers: Assessing First and Second Language Development*, provides helpful, culturally sensitive insights on recognizing how children are learning and performing and how teachers can assist in that process.

CDE Press
P.O. Box 271
Sacramento, CA 95812-0217
(800) 995-4099
FAX (916) 323-0823
http://www.cde.ca.gov/cdepress/

DEC Recommended Practices in Early Intervention/Early Childhood Special Education
Edited by S. Sandall, M. E. McLean, & B. J. Smith (2000)

This document is a good and current source of information about recommended practices and strategies for using them. Chapter 2 ("Recommended Practices in Assessment"), by John T. Neisworth and Stephen J. Bagnato, offers definitions of terms, delineation of quality features, and a checklist for personal or program assessment practices.

Sopris West
4093 Specialty Place
Longmont, CO 80504
(800) 547-6747
FAX (888) 819-7767
http://www.sopriswest.com

It Matters: Lessons From My Son
by J. Fialka (1997)

The poems in this book speak directly and honestly from parent to parent and parent to professional about what works and what doesn't. In particular, "The Label," "On Having to Give Bad News," and "Advice to Professionals Who Must 'Conference Cases'" should be read by every family and professional, again and again.

> Janice Fialka
> 10474 La Salle Boulevard
> Huntington Woods, MI 48070
> (248) 546-4870
> ruaw@aol.com

New Visions for the Developmental Assessment of Infants and Young Children
Edited by S. J. Meisels & E. Fenichel (1996)

This book offers clear and current rethinking of the key issues from five perspectives, one of which is the family point of view. Cultural considerations, information gathering strategies, and policy considerations also are addressed.

> Paul H. Brookes Publishing
> P.O. Box 10624
> Baltimore, MD 21285-0624
> (800) 638-3775
> FAX (410) 337-8539
> http://www.pbrookes.com

One Child, Two Languages: A Guide for Preschool Educators of Children Learning English as a Second Language
by P. O. Tabors (1997)

Help for early childhood educators in understanding the process of second language acquisition in young children is what this book provides, as well as organizational and curricular strategies for developing supportive environments for young, diverse language learners. Based on extensive research, the author offers a variety of resources, including vignettes, teaching cases, classroom observations, suggestions for teaching/training, and strategies for involving parents.

> Paul H. Brookes Publishing
> P.O. Box 10624
> Baltimore, MD 21285-0624
> (800) 638-3775
> FAX (410) 337-8539
> http://www.pbrookes.com

Reach for the Stars, Plan for the Future
by J. Grisham-Brown & D. G. Haynes (1999)

This is a first-of-its-kind guidebook about building on the assessment process to create strengths-based plans for young children. The strategies and forms provided are designed to help families imagine positive and productive futures and to support steps toward those futures through planning with program personnel.

> American Printing House for the Blind
> P.O. Box 6085
> Louisville, KY 40206-0085
> (800) 223-1839
> FAX (502) 899-2274
> http://www.aph.org/

Transdisciplinary Play-Based Assessment
by T. W. Linder (1993)

Creative strategies for gathering information about young children (0-6) using natural play interactions are offered in this monograph. The book contains observation guidelines and worksheets for identifying a child's strengths, needs, and areas of concern in cognitive, social-emotional, communication, and sensorimotor domains.

> Paul H. Brookes Publishing
> P.O. Box 10624
> Baltimore, MD 21285-0624
> (800) 638-3775
> FAX (410) 337-8539
> http://www.pbrookes.com

Transdisciplinary Play-Based Intervention
by T. W. Linder (1993)

Transdisciplinary strategies for promoting cognitive, social-emotional, communication, and sensorimotor development are the strength of this resource. It offers a "Transdisciplinary Play-Based Intervention (TPBI) Planner" to support team members in designing and implementing individualized family service plans and education programs.

> Paul H. Brookes Publishing
> P.O. Box 10624
> Baltimore, MD 21285-0624
> (800) 638-3775
> FAX (410) 337-8539
> http://www.pbrookes.com

Videotapes

Breaking the News
by the Institute for Families of Blind Children (1990)

Don't be put off by the fact that this resource was developed for pediatric ophthalmologists! It's a short, powerful videotape (15 minutes) on the challenges of sharing difficult diagnostic information sensitively. The section on sharing information with compassion is particularly strong.

Institute for Families of Blind Children
P.O. Box 54700
Mail Stop 111
Los Angeles, CA 90054-0700
(323) 669-4649
FAX (323) 665-7869
http://www.instituteforfamilies.org

But He Knows His Colors: Characteristics of Autism in Children Birth to Three
by C. McClain & P. Osbourn (1993)

The purpose of this videotape is to teach families, educators, early interventionists, and other practitioners about the spectrum of characteristics seen in young children with autism. It provides the opportunity to observe four children, all under the age of three, in a variety of settings and assessment situations.

Child Health and Development Media, Inc. (CHADEM)
5632 Van Nuys Boulevard, Suite 286
Van Nuys, CA 91401
(800) 405-8942
FAX (818) 989-7826
http://www.childdevmedia.com

First Years Together: Involving Parents in Infant Assessment
by Project Enlightenment (1989)

This 19-minute videotape accomplishes several purposes. It provides parent perspectives on what they like and do not like about assessment procedures. It demonstrates professionals collaborating with family members in formal and informal assessment situations. It also demonstrates using assessment as an opportunity to plan interventions and support parent strengths and accomplishments.

Project Enlightenment Publications
501 South Boylan Avenue
Raleigh, NC 27603
(919) 856-7778
FAX (919) 508-0810

Improving the Post-Assessment Process: Families and Teams Together
by S. M. Moore, A. Ferguson, & W. Eiserman (1995)

Comments from family members and professionals about effective family-centered approaches to post-assessment information sharing and intervention planning form the core of this video.

Western Media Products
P.O. Box 591
Denver, CO 80201
(303) 455-4177
FAX (303) 455-5302
http://www.media-products.com

A Three-Way Conversation: Effective Use of Cultural Mediators, Interpreters, and Translators
by the Spectrum Project and Project A.C.T. (1999)

Cultural mediators, interpreters, and translators are essential to the participation of culturally and linguistically diverse young children and families in the assessment process. This videotape explores the effective use of these resources, offering comments and insights from both parents and service providers. The brief vignette on communication provides a "wake-up call" with regard to culturally appropriate assessment. Clips are paired with thought-provoking questions to promote discussion.

Western Media Products
P.O. Box 591
Denver, CO 80201
(800) 232-8902
FAX (303) 455-5302
http://www.media-products.com

Transdisciplinary Arena Assessment Process: A Resource for Teams
by Child Development Resources, Inc. (1992)

This 43-minute videotape demonstrates a six-step family-centered transdisciplinary approach to arena assessment and individualized family support plan (IFSP) development. The accompanying viewing guide provides an overview of the transdisciplinary approach and a summary of the process, as well as supporting activities and supplemental materials.

Child Development Resources (CDR)
P.O. Box 280
Norge, VA 23127-0280
(757) 566-3300
FAX (757) 566-8977
http://www.cdr.org

Web Resources

Early Identification
National Early Childhood Technical Assistance Center

The National Early Childhood Technical Assistance Center has compiled a variety of helpful and informative resources at this site. Publications on key topics (e.g., eligibility, informed clinical opinion), information from funded projects, and examples of state assessment practices are examples of what's available.

    http://www.nectac.org/topics/earlyid/earlyid.asp

How Can I Assess the Development of My Preschooler?
LD Online

This brochure describes areas of development that parents can assess, thoughts on when a parent should seek professional help with assessment, and resources for more information.

    http://www.ldonline.org/ld_indepth/early_identification/parent_brochure.html

New Visions for Parents
Zero to Three: National Center for Infants, Toddlers, and Families

The helpful resources available through this Web site include a letter for parents (about developmental assessment), a guidebook (*New Visions: A Parent's Guide to Understanding Developmental Assessment*), information on preparing for the assessment process, and a list of frequently used terms.

    http://www.zerotothree.org/parent.html?Load=parent_intro.html

Recommended Practices for Assessment in Early Childhood Settings (Birth to Eight Years)
National Early Childhood Technical Assistance Center

This site's 51 PowerPoint slides from an April 2001 presentation by John T. Neisworth and Stephen J. Bagnato are a rich resource on assessment. Links to other assessment resources by these authors are provided.

    http://www.nectac.org/topics/earlyid/RecPractices/RecAssessSlides/sld001.htm

Statewide Readiness Assessment
National Early Childhood Technical Assistance Center

A range of resources (e.g., position statements, articles, conference proceedings, Web sites) on readiness, an evolving aspect of assessment, is available at this site.

http://www.nectac.org/topics/readiassess/readiassess.asp

Using Accommodations in the Assessment of Young Children With Disabilities
California Institute on Human Services, Sonoma State University

The strategies offered at this site are designed to assist teachers in structuring environments in which young children with disabilities can show what they know and can do. This is a nice resource to use when thinking about how to maximize assessment outcomes.

http://www.regionvqnet.org/qnet/research/RI2002/pdfs/MMarticle.pdf

DEC Recommended Practices

in Early Intervention/Early Childhood Special Education

Bridging the gap between research and practice, the book *DEC Recommended Practices* provides guidance on effective practices for working with young children with disabilities. The recommended practices are based on a review and synthesis of the research literature and the practices identified as critical by various stakeholders in early intervention/early childhood special education.

The book contains recommended practices in the following areas:

- Assessment—*John Neisworth and Stephen Bagnato*
- Child-focused interventions—*Mark Wolery*
- Family-based practices—*Carol Trivette and Carl Dunst*
- Interdisciplinary models—*R.A. McWilliam*
- Technology applications—*Kathleen Stremel*
- Policies, procedures, and systems change—*Gloria Harbin and Christine Salisbury*
- Personnel preparation—*Patricia Miller and Vicki Stayton*

In *DEC Recommended Practices*, you'll learn about the connection between early learning experiences and later school and work performance and how to bring those practices together to help educators, other practitioners, families, and administrators give children with disabilities quality learning experiences.

G143REC

SOPRIS WEST
EDUCATIONAL SERVICES

Phone: (800) 547-6747
Fax: (888) 819-7767
www.sopriswest.com

NEW from
Sopris West and DEC!

Video: **Selected Strategies for Teaching Young Children With Special Needs**

This video demonstrates environments and several teaching procedures from *DEC Recommended Practices in Early Intervention/Early Childhood Special Education* (Sandall, McLean, & Smith, 2000), including:

- Peer-mediated strategies
- Using consequences
- Prompting strategies
- Naturalistic teaching procedures
- Environments that promote learning

These effective strategies are based on an extensive literature review and focus groups of parents, teachers, and administrators about what promotes learning for young children with special needs.

SOPRIS WEST
EDUCATIONAL SERVICES

Phone: (800) 547-6747
Fax: (888) 819-7767
www.sopriswest.com

Young Exceptional Children is **unique** and **practical!** *It is designed for any adult who works or lives with a young child who has a disability, developmental delay, special gifts or talents, or other special needs.*

Young Exceptional Children (YEC) is a peer-reviewed publication produced four times per year by the Division for Early Childhood (DEC) of the Council for Exceptional Children (CEC) with practical ideas for early childhood teachers, therapists, parents, and administrators. Topics include: challenging behaviors, family-guided routines, developmentally appropriate practices for children with special needs, best practices for young children with autism, strategies for successful inclusion, practical ideas for parents and professionals to promote learning and development, and more!